D0954581

PARAMAHANSA YOGANANDA
(1893 – 1952)

Where There Is LIGHT

Insight and Inspiration
for Meeting Life's Challenges

Selections from the teachings of

PARAMAHANSA YOGANANDA

Self-Realization Fellowship
FOUNDED 1920
Paramahansa Yogananda

ABOUT THIS BOOK: The excerpts from the teachings of Parama-hansa Yogananda in this compilation originally appeared in his books, articles in *Self-Realization* (the magazine he founded in 1925), and other Self-Realization Fellowship publications. The selections included here were chosen from Sri Yogananda's writings, lectures, and informal talks to provide a convenient compendium of quotations—one to which readers could quickly turn for encouraging and enlightening counsel on a variety of subjects. *Where There Is Light* has found a wide and appreciative audience since it was first published in 1988.

 Authorized by the International Publications Council of
SELF-REALIZATION FELLOWSHIP

The Self-Realization Fellowship name and emblem (shown above) appear on all SRF books, recordings, and other publications, assuring the reader that a work originates with the society established by Paramahansa Yogananda and faithfully conveys his teachings.

Library of Congress Catalog Number: 88-063330

ISBN 0-87612-720-0 (paperback)
ISBN-13 978-0-87612-720-9 (paperback)

Printed in the United States of America

1676-J5629

Contents

Note to the Third Edition (2015)   x

Preface, *by Sri Daya Mata*   xi

Introduction.   xiii

Chapter

1. Our Infinite Potential **3**

2. Strength in Times of Adversity **11**

3. Learn to Meditate **21**

     Meditation: The Most Practical Science   21

     Preparatory Instructions   22

     A Preliminary Breathing Exercise   23

     Concentrate on the Peace and Joy of the Soul . .   24

     The Deeper Yoga Science of Meditation.   26

     A Guided Meditation Exercise   27

     A Meditation on Peace   27

     Meditate Until You Feel the Divine Response . .   29

4. Rising Above Suffering. **30**

     The Healing Power of God   36

     The Power of Affirmation and Prayer.   38

     Technique of Affirmation   40

     Cultivating Faith in God   44

5. Security in an Uncertain World. **50**

6. Wisdom to Solve Problems and Make Life's Decisions. **57**

     Developing Discriminative Judgment   59

     Intuition: Insight of the Soul.   64

7. Achieving Your Goals **67**

     Using Dynamic Will Power.   67

Dealing Constructively With Failure 70
Concentration: A Key to Success 73
Creativity 75
Creating All-Round Success 78
The Value of Enthusiasm 80
Abundance and Prosperity. 83

8. **Inner Peace: Antidote for Stress, Worry, and Fear. 87**

Nervousness. 88
Worry and Fear. 91

9. **Bringing Out the Best Within You 100**

Introspection: A Secret of Progress 102
Conquering Temptations. 104
The Correct Attitude Toward Past Wrongs 110
Creating Good Habits and Destroying Bad Ones . 114

10. **Happiness 120**

Positive Mental Attitudes 120
Freedom From Negative Moods 125
Service to Others 129
The Inner Conditions of Happiness 130

11. **Getting Along With Others 135**

Dealing With Inharmonious Relationships 135
Developing a Harmonious Personality. 138
Overcoming Negative Emotions. 141
Forgiveness. 146

12. **Unconditional Love: Perfecting Human Relationships 150**

Balancing Feminine and Masculine Qualities . . 152
Marriage 155
Friendship. 160

13. **Understanding Death. 166**

**14. How to Use Thoughts of Immortality to
Awaken Your True Self** **178**

Day and Night, Affirm What You Really Are . . 178
Peel Away All Limiting Thoughts 179
Know Your Self as Inseparable From God 180
Think, Affirm, Realize Your Divine Nature ... 181
Impress the Mind With Divine Truth 182
Your Soul Cannot Be Harmed by Trials 184
Fear Nothing, for You Are a Child of God 185
You Are Spirit: Affirm Your Spiritual Qualities 186
You Are Light, You Are Joy 187
You Are Love 189
"Thou Art That" 190

15. The Consummate Goal **192**

Making Time for God in Your Life 194
Practicing the Presence of God 198
Establishing a Relationship With God 203
Proof of God's Response 204
The Personal Element in the Search for God... 207

About the Author 215

Glossary................................. 224

Index 235

The Spiritual Legacy of Paramahansa Yogananda

His Complete Writings, Lectures, and Informal Talks

Paramahansa Yogananda founded Self-Realization Fellowship in 1920 to disseminate his teachings worldwide and to preserve their purity and integrity for generations to come. A prolific writer and lecturer from his earliest years in America, he created a renowned and voluminous body of works on the yoga science of meditation, the art of balanced living, and the underlying unity of all great religions. Today this unique and far-reaching spiritual legacy lives on, inspiring millions of truth-seekers all over the world.

In accord with the express wishes of the great master, Self-Realization Fellowship has continued the ongoing task of publishing and keeping permanently in print *The Complete Works of Paramahansa Yogananda*. These include not only the final editions of all the books he published during his lifetime, but also many new titles — works that had remained unpublished at the time of his passing in 1952, or which had been serialized over the years in incomplete form in Self-Realization Fellowship's magazine, as well as hundreds of profoundly inspiring lectures and informal talks recorded but not printed before his passing.

Paramahansa Yogananda personally chose and trained those close disciples who formed the Self-Realization Fellowship Publications Council, giving them specific guidelines for the preparation and publishing of his teachings. The members of the SRF Publications Council (monks and nuns who have taken lifelong vows of renunciation and selfless service) honor these guidelines as a sacred trust, in order that the universal message of this beloved world teacher will live on in its original power and authenticity.

The Self-Realization Fellowship emblem (shown above) was designated by Paramahansa Yogananda to identify the nonprofit society he founded as the authorized source of his teachings. The SRF name and emblem appear on all Self-Realization Fellowship publications and recordings, assuring the reader that a work originates with the organization founded by Paramahansa Yogananda and conveys his teachings as he himself intended they be given.

SELF-REALIZATION FELLOWSHIP

Note to the Third Edition
(2015)

In the nearly thirty years since its first publication, *Where There Is Light* has been well received as a popular overview and introduction to the spiritual teachings of Paramahansa Yogananda. Translated into many languages, it has found an enduring place in the lives of countless readers of *Autobiography of a Yogi* and other works by him.

This new edition includes two new chapters: "Learn to Meditate" (chapter 3) and "How to Use Thoughts of Immortality to Awaken Your True Self" (chapter 14). Both of these new chapters offer practical methods by which readers can put into immediate practice the insights and inspiration from Paramahansa Yogananda's teachings found throughout this book. Other chapters have been revised to accommodate additional quotations from works by him that had not yet been published when *Where There Is Light* was first released in 1988.

May this new edition bring light and hope to the ever-growing number of souls who are turning to the writings of this beloved world teacher as a beacon of universal and all-inclusive spiritual guidance for our emerging world civilization.

SELF-REALIZATION FELLOWSHIP

Preface

BY SRI DAYA MATA

President and spiritual head (1955–2010) of Self-Realization Fellowship/Yogoda Satsanga Society of India

During the years in which I was blessed to receive the spiritual training of Paramahansa Yogananda,* I came to see that the mark of true wisdom is twofold: First, it encompasses every aspect of our being—body, mind, and soul; our personal lives as well as our relationships with family, community, and the world. At the same time, it is so simple and direct that we inwardly feel, "Yes, of course! I have always known that!" There is a sense of reawakening to an understanding that was already present within. When we are touched on this deeper level, truth is instantly translated from mere philosophy into active, workable solutions to our problems.

Such were the truths that flowed in a ceaseless stream from my guru, Paramahansa Yogananda—not as theological abstractions or platitudes, but as practical expressions of that supreme wisdom which brings success, health, enduring happiness, and divine love into all the circumstances of life. Though the full range and depth of Paramahansaji's† teachings fills many volumes, we are pleased to present in this compilation a few of the individual gems of thought that sparkle throughout his writings and lectures—profound truths conveyed in a few potent words

---

* Sri Daya Mata entered the Self-Realization Fellowship ashram as a monastic in 1931, and received spiritual training directly from Paramahansa Yogananda for over twenty years. She was chosen by him to be the third president and representative spiritual head of his worldwide society, a position she held from 1955 to her passing in 2010.

† *Ji* is a suffix denoting respect.

that kindle a renewed awareness of our limitless inner resources, and that provide a reassuring sense of direction in times of uncertainty or crisis.

It was these innate capabilities of strength and intuitive understanding that Paramahansa Yogananda endeavored to awaken in those who sought his training. When difficulties arose in our personal lives or in the affairs of his worldwide society, we would hasten to him for a solution. However, it often happened that before we even had a chance to say anything, he would motion for us to sit and meditate. In his presence, our minds became calm and centered in God; and the restlessness and confusion created by our problems were completely dissolved. Even if he said nothing in answer to our questions, when we returned to our duties our thoughts formed more clearly, and we discovered that something within us had discerned the right way to proceed.

Paramahansaji gave us a solid grounding in the principles needed to guide our thoughts and actions with wisdom, courage, and faith. But he didn't do our thinking for us; he insisted that we develop our own discrimination by deepening our attunement with God, so that we could perceive for ourselves the best course of action in any particular situation.

It is my deepest hope that each reader will find in this sampling of Paramahansa Yogananda's words the wisdom and inspiration to chart a victorious path through the challenging circumstances of his or her own life. Above all, may these truths bring a lasting incentive to seek those inner resources of strength, joy, and love that spring from our eternal relationship with God. For in that discovery lies the highest fulfillment life can bring.

DAYA MATA

Los Angeles, California
December 1988

Introduction

"In seemingly empty space there is one Link, one Life eternal, which unites everything in the universe—animate and inanimate—one wave of Life flowing through everything."

—*Paramahansa Yogananda*

As our world civilization progresses, our greatest cause for optimism is the emerging recognition of the underlying oneness of life. Humanity's loftiest spiritual traditions have taught for centuries that our lives are integral parts of a universal whole; today they are being joined by physicists, the new "visionaries," who are proclaiming that one cord of unity links the farthest galaxies with the smallest cells of our bodies. And as their findings begin to coalesce with those of biology, medicine, psychology, ecology, and other fields, we find ourselves poised on the brink of a revolution in human understanding—catching glimpses of a unity and harmony so vast, so breathtakingly perfect, that we are left with a radically different view of ourselves and our potentials.

This new vision offers a deep sense of reassurance in the face of the profound challenges confronting our world today. We are beginning to see that we are not helpless victims of a randomly chaotic cosmos. Diseases of body and mind; the equally alarming "dis-eases" affecting our family, social, and economic stability; the ecological threats to the earth itself—all these arise from a lack of accord with the essential harmony and unity of the cosmos, whether on the personal, community, national, or planetary level. By learning to integrate our lives with this universal harmony, we can victoriously meet any challenge to our well-being.*

Our age has been the recipient of an unprecedented number of theories and methods for achieving that well-being. Medicine, psychology, and the burgeoning number of metaphysical approaches all offer solutions from their specialized perspectives; but the resulting avalanche of information, much of it seemingly contradictory, often leaves us unable to discern a continuity, an order that gives focus to our efforts to help ourselves and others. We find ourselves yearning for a larger perspective, some way of harmonizing and transcending the partial views resulting from our era's overspecialization.

That larger perspective — anciently discovered by the founders of the world's great spiritual traditions and newly glimpsed by pioneering scientists of modern times — reveals that underlying both science and religion are universal principles that govern all creation. "Science looks at truth only from without," Paramahansa Yogananda said. "The metaphysician looks at truth from within to without. That is why they clash. But realized souls who understand science as well as metaphysics find no difference at all. They see the parallelism between science and truth because they see the whole picture."

---

* "The cosmic order that upholds the universe is not different from the moral order that rules man's destiny," wrote Paramahansa Yogananda. Modern science is increasingly confirming the efficacy of India's ancient methods of bringing human consciousness into balanced harmony with cosmic laws, as evidenced by this recent comment from Professor Brian D. Josephson, winner of the Nobel Prize in physics: "The Vedanta and Sankhya [systems of Hindu philosophy of which Yoga is the practical application] hold the key to the laws of mind and thought process, which are correlated to the quantum field, i.e., the operation and distribution of particles at atomic and molecular levels."

Paramahansa Yogananda's lifework* was to show how each of us can transform that vision of harmony from an intellectual possibility into direct personal experience that is applicable to our daily lives. A world teacher who brought the ancient science of yoga meditation† to the West in 1920, he dedicated his life to uniting East and West in the lasting ties of spiritual understanding, and to helping others toward realization of the infinite resources of peace, love, and joy that exist within every human being.

Where There Is Light contains but a small sampling of his teachings. The diverse flavor of its contents reflects the wide spectrum of sources from which they are drawn: Some passages are taken from public lectures or classes; others come from informal talks to small groups of disciples and friends; additional selections are from his writings.

A more detailed discussion of the principles referred to in the present volume can be found in the publications listed on page 222. For readers unfamiliar with the philosophy and spiritual ideals of Paramahansa Yogananda, *Where There Is Light* will serve as a useful introduction. And for all who have begun the inner journey toward the Source of that light, this compilation is offered as a handbook of spiritual counsel—a unique resource of insight and inspiration for daily life.

SELF-REALIZATION FELLOWSHIP

---

* See "About the Author," page 215.
† See *yoga* in glossary.

WHERE THERE IS LIGHT

CHAPTER 1

Our Infinite Potential

When we begin to understand the total being that is man, we realize that he is no simple physical organism. Within him are many powers whose potential he employs in greater or lesser degree in accommodating himself to the conditions of this world. Their potential is vastly greater than the average person thinks.

❖ ❖ ❖

Behind the light in every little bulb is a great dynamic current; beneath every little wave is the vast ocean, which has become the many waves. So it is with human beings. God made every man in His image,* and gave each one freedom. But you forget the Source of your being and the unequaled power of God that is an inherent part of you. The possibilities of this world are limitless; the potential progress of man is limitless.

❖ ❖ ❖

Every human being is an expression of the great, vast Spirit. Since you are a manifestation of Spirit, you should make an effort to express your infinite potentialities.

❖ ❖ ❖

* Genesis 1:27.

3

What you are is much greater than anything or anyone else you have ever yearned for. God is manifest in you in a way that He is not manifest in any other human being. Your face is unlike anyone else's, your soul is unlike anyone else's, you are sufficient unto yourself; for within your soul lies the greatest treasure of all—God.

❖ ❖ ❖

All great teachers declare that within this body is the immortal soul, a spark of That which sustains all.

❖ ❖ ❖

Whence does our true personality derive? It comes from God. He is Absolute Consciousness, Absolute Existence, and Absolute Bliss....By concentrating within, you can directly feel the divine bliss of your soul within and also without. If you can stabilize yourself in that consciousness, your outer personality will develop and become attractive to all beings. The soul is made in God's image, and when we become established in soul awareness, our personality begins to reflect His goodness and beauty. That is your real personality. Any other characteristics you display are more or less a graft—they are not the real "you."

❖ ❖ ❖

Analyze yourself: Something within you is always prodding you to seek that "something else" which seems to be missing in your life. In the inner self of all human beings is a deep-seated need for achievement. Why? Because we have fallen away from the Father's bosom. We have wandered away from our eternal home in God, and we long to regain that lost perfection.

❖ ❖ ❖

The soul is absolutely perfect, but when identified with the body as ego,* its expression becomes distorted by human imperfections....Yoga teaches us to know the divine nature in ourselves and others. Through yoga meditation we can know that we are gods.†

❖ ❖ ❖

The moon's reflection cannot be seen clearly in ruffled water, but when the water's surface is calm a perfect reflection of the moon appears. So with the mind: when it is calm you see clearly reflected the moonèd face of the soul. As souls we are reflections of God. When by meditation techniques‡ we withdraw restless thoughts from the lake of the mind, we behold our soul, a perfect reflection of Spirit, and realize that the soul and God are One.

---

* See *egoism* in glossary.

† "I have said, Ye are gods; and all of you are children of the Most High"(Psalms 82:6). "Is it not written in your law, I said, Ye are gods?" (John 10:34).

‡ "Be still, and know that I am God" (Psalms 46:10). Scientific techniques of yoga meditation that enable one to calm and interiorize the consciousness and perceive God's presence within are taught by Paramahansa Yogananda in the *Self-Realization Fellowship Lessons,* a comprehensive home-study series compiled from his classes and lectures and available from Self-Realization Fellowship International Headquarters.

❖ ❖ ❖

Self-realization* is the knowing—in body, mind, and soul—that we are one with the omnipresence of God; that we do not have to pray that it come to us, that we are not merely near it at all times, but that God's omnipresence is our omnipresence; that we are just as much a part of Him now as we ever will be. All we have to do is improve our knowing.

❖ ❖ ❖

Focus your attention within.† You will feel a new power, a new strength, a new peace—in body, mind and spirit....By communing with God you change your status from a mortal being to an immortal being. When you do this, all bonds that limit you will be broken.

❖ ❖ ❖

Mines of power lie unexplored within you. You use this power unconsciously in all things you do, and you achieve certain results; but, if you learn how to consciously control and use the powers within you, you can accomplish much more.

❖ ❖ ❖

Few people in this world try consciously to develop the potentials of body, mind, and soul. The rest are victims of circumstances of the past. They plod

* See *Self* in glossary.

† "Neither shall they say, Lo here! or, lo there! for, behold, the kingdom of God is within you" (Luke 17:21).

on and on, pushed by past wrong habits, helplessly going down under their influence, remembering only: "I am a nervous man," or "I am a weakling," or "I am a sinner," and so on.

It lies with each one of us to cut with the sword of wisdom the cords of our bondage, or to remain bound.

❖ ❖ ❖

One of the illusions of life is to continue to live helplessly. As soon as you say, "It's no use," it becomes so....To think you cannot change at will is delusion.

❖ ❖ ❖

Our little minds are part of the omnipotent mind of God. Beneath the wave of our consciousness is the infinite ocean of His consciousness. It is because the wave forgets it is a part of the Ocean that it becomes isolated from that oceanic power. As a result, our minds have become weakened by our trials and material limitations. The mind has stopped its work. You will be surprised how much it can do if you cast off the limitations you have put on it.

❖ ❖ ❖

Why limit your capability to the adage, "Don't bite off more than you can chew"? I believe you should bite off more than you can chew, and then chew it!

❖ ❖ ❖

The mind is like an elastic band. The more you

pull, the more it stretches. The mind-elastic will never break. Every time you feel limitations, close your eyes and say to yourself, "I am the Infinite," and you will see what power you have.

❖ ❖ ❖

When you say to me that you can't do this or that, I don't believe it. Whatever you make up your mind to do, you can do. God is the sum total of everything, and His image is within you. He can do anything, and so can you, if you learn to identify yourself with His inexhaustible nature.

❖ ❖ ❖

Don't look on yourself as a weak mortal. Incredible amounts of energy are hidden in your brain; enough in a gram of flesh to run the city of Chicago for two days.* And you say you are tired?

❖ ❖ ❖

God made us angels of energy, encased in solids — currents of life dazzling through a material bulb of flesh. But through concentration on the frailties and fragility of the body bulb, we have forgotten how to feel the immortal, indestructible properties of the eternal life energy within the mutable flesh.

❖ ❖ ❖

---

* Centuries before modern physicists proved the equivalence of matter and energy, India's sages proclaimed that every material form is reducible to patterns of energy. See *prana* in glossary.

When you go beyond the consciousness of this world, knowing that you are not the body or the mind, and yet aware as never before that you exist—that divine consciousness is what you are. You are That in which is rooted everything in the universe.

❖ ❖ ❖

You are all gods, if you only knew it. Behind the wave of your consciousness is the sea of God's presence. You must look within. Don't concentrate on the little wave of the body with its weaknesses; look beneath....As you lift your consciousness from the body and its experiences, you will find that sphere [of your consciousness] filled with the great joy and bliss that lights the stars and gives power to the winds and storms. God is the source of all our joys and of all the manifestations in nature....

Awaken yourself from the gloom of ignorance. You have closed your eyes in the sleep of delusion.* Awake! Open your eyes and you shall behold the glory of God—the vast vista of God's light spreading over all things. I am telling you to be divine realists, and you will find the answer to all questions in God.

Affirmations†

I am submerged in eternal light. It permeates

---

* See *maya* in glossary.

† Instructions for using affirmations are given on pages 38 ff.

every particle of my being. I am living in that light. The Divine Spirit fills me within and without.

❖ ❖ ❖

O Father, break the boundaries of the little waves of my life that I may join the ocean of Thy vastness.

CHAPTER 2

Strength in Times of Adversity

Everything the Lord has created is to try us, to bring out the buried soul immortality within us. That is the adventure of life, the one purpose of life. And everyone's adventure is different, unique. You should be prepared to deal with all problems of health, mind, and soul by commonsense methods and faith in God, knowing that in life or death your soul remains unconquered.

❖ ❖ ❖

Never let life beat you down. Beat life! If you have a strong will you can overcome all difficulties. Affirm, even in the midst of trials: "Danger and I were born together, and I am more dangerous than danger!" This is a truth you should always remember; apply it and you will see that it works. Don't behave like a cringing mortal being. You are a child of God!

❖ ❖ ❖

Many people are afraid of life's problems. I have never feared them, for I have always prayed: "Lord, may Thy power increase in me. Keep me in the positive consciousness that with Thy help I can always overcome my difficulties."

❖ ❖ ❖

Since you are made in God's image, to believe that your tests are more difficult than your divinity is powerful to overcome them is to believe in an untruth. Remember, no matter what your tests are, you are not too weak to fight. God will not suffer you to be tempted more than you are able to bear.

❖ ❖ ❖

Saint Francis had more troubles than you could imagine, but he didn't give up. One by one, by the power of mind, he overcame those obstacles and became one with the Master of the Universe. Why shouldn't you have that kind of determination?

❖ ❖ ❖

Use every trial that comes to you as an opportunity to improve yourself. When you are passing through the difficulties and tests of life, you usually become rebellious: "Why should this happen to me?" Instead, you should think of every trial as a pickax with which to dig into the soil of your consciousness and release the fountain of spiritual strength that lies within. Each test should bring out the hidden power that is within you as a child of God, made in His image.

❖ ❖ ❖

To fly away from problems may seem the easiest solution. But you gain strength only when you wrestle with a strong opponent. One who doesn't have difficulties is one who doesn't grow.

❖ ❖ ❖

A life without problems would be no life at all—with no incentive to improve ourselves and develop our divine potential.

❖ ❖ ❖

To be a conqueror of self is to be truly victorious—to conquer your circumscribed consciousness and expand your spiritual powers without limit. You can go as far as you want to go, past all limitations, and live a supremely victorious existence.

Break out of the mental cell of ignorance that has you confined. Think differently.

❖ ❖ ❖

With the thought-sword of wisdom, destroy the thought-cords that bind you. Life is a battle and you must fight to win it....Who can stop you from thinking you are a god? No one. You are your only obstruction.

❖ ❖ ❖

You must cease to think you are a mortal being if you would find lasting happiness. Practice this truth in your daily life.

❖ ❖ ❖

Smile at the world with a smile from within.... Learn to be happy at will and to hold on to that happiness within, no matter what happens. Some people are absolutely crushed by their tests; others smile on in spite of their difficulties. Those who are unconquered in spirit are the real successes in life.

❖ ❖ ❖

When my trials become very great, I first seek understanding in myself. I don't blame circumstances or try to correct anybody else. I go inside first. I try to clean the citadel of my soul to remove anything that obstructs the soul's all-powerful, all-wise expression. That is the successful way to live.

❖ ❖ ❖

Trouble and disease have a lesson for us. Our painful experiences are not meant to destroy us, but to burn out our dross, to hurry us back Home. No one is more anxious for our release than God.

❖ ❖ ❖

The smoke-screen of delusion has come between us and God, and He is sorry that we have lost sight of Him. He is not happy seeing His children suffer so much—dying from falling bombs, terrible diseases, and wrong habits of living. He regrets it, for He loves us and wants us back. If only you would make the effort at night to meditate and be with Him! He thinks of you so much. You are not forsaken. It is you who have forsaken your Self.

❖ ❖ ❖

When you use life's experiences as your teacher, and learn from them the true nature of the world and your part in it, those experiences become valuable guides to eternal fulfillment and happiness.

❖ ❖ ❖

In a sense misery is your best friend, because it starts you seeking God. When you begin to see clearly the imperfection of the world, you will begin to seek the perfection of God. The truth is that God is using evil, not to destroy us, but to make us disillusioned with His toys, with the playthings of this world, so that we might seek Him.

❖ ❖ ❖

Gloom is but the shade of Divine Mother's* hand outstretched caressingly. Don't forget that. Sometimes, when the Mother is going to caress you, a shadow is caused by Her hand before it touches you. So when trouble comes, don't think that She is punishing you; Her hand overshadowing you holds some blessing as it reaches out to bring you nearer to Her.

❖ ❖ ❖

Suffering is a good teacher to those who are quick and willing to learn from it. But it becomes a tyrant to those who resist and resent. Suffering can teach us almost everything. Its lessons urge us to develop discrimination, self-control, nonattachment, morality, and transcendent spiritual consciousness. For example, a stomachache tells us not to eat too much and to watch what we eat. The pain from loss of possessions

---

* The scriptures of India teach that God is both personal and impersonal, immanent and transcendent. Seekers in the West have traditionally related to God in His personal aspect as Father; in India, the concept of God as the loving, compassionate Mother of the Universe has widespread appeal. See *Divine Mother* in glossary.

or loved ones reminds us of the temporal nature of all things in this world of delusion. The consequences of wrong actions impel us to exercise discrimination. Why not learn through wisdom? Then you won't subject yourself to unnecessary painful discipline from the hard taskmaster of suffering.

❖ ❖ ❖

Suffering is caused by the misuse of free will. God has given us the power to accept Him or reject Him. He doesn't want us to encounter woes, but will not interfere when we choose actions that lead to misery.

❖ ❖ ❖

All the causes of ill health or sudden financial failure or other troubles that come upon you without warning, and without your knowing why, were created by you in the past, in this or in previous incarnations, and have been silently germinating in your consciousness....* Don't blame God or anyone else if you are suffering from disease, financial problems, emotional upsets. You created the cause of the problem in the past and must make a greater determination to uproot it now.

❖ ❖ ❖

Too many people misinterpret the meaning of

---

* Reincarnation, the soul's evolutionary journey back to God, provides repeated opportunities for growth, achievement, and fulfillment not possible in one brief lifespan of earthly existence. See glossary.

karma,* adopting a fatalistic attitude. You do not have to accept karma. If I tell you that somebody is standing behind you ready to hurt you because you once hit him, and you meekly say, "Well, it is my karma," and wait for him to strike you, of course you will get a blow! Why don't you try to mollify him? By pacifying him you may lessen his bitterness and remove his desire to strike you.

❖ ❖ ❖

The effects of your actions have much less power to hurt you when you do not allow the mind to give in to them. Remember that. You can also resist by counteracting the bad effects of past wrong actions with good effects set in motion by present right actions, thus preventing the creation of an environment favorable to the fruition of your bad karma.

❖ ❖ ❖

When you realize yourself as a child of God, what karma have you? God has no karma. And you have none, when you *know* you are His child. Every day you should affirm, "I am not a mortal being; I am not the body. I am a child of God." That is practicing the presence of God. God is free from karma. You are made in His image. You also are free from karma.

❖ ❖ ❖

* The results of past actions, governed by the law of cause and effect. "Whatsoever a man soweth, that shall he also reap" (Galatians 6:7). See glossary.

Let nobody tell you your suffering or problems are your karma. You [the soul] have no karma. Shankara* said: "I am one with Spirit; I am He." If you *realize* this truth, you are a god. But if you keep mentally affirming, "I am a god," and in the background of your mind you are thinking, "But it seems I am a mortal being," you are a mortal being. If you *know* you are a god, you are free.

❖ ❖ ❖

"Know ye not that ye are the temple of God, and that the Spirit of God dwelleth in you?"† If you can clarify and expand your mind through meditation, and receive God in your consciousness, you too will be free from the delusion of disease, limitations, and death.

❖ ❖ ❖

If you want to rise above karma, try to realize these three truths: (1) *When the mind is strong and the heart is pure, you are free.* It is the mind that connects you with pain in the body. When you think pure thoughts and are mentally strong, you cannot suffer the painful effects of evil karma. This is something very cheerful I have found. (2) *In subconscious sleep, you are free.* (3) *When you are in ecstasy,*‡

---

* Swami Shankara was one of India's most illustrious philosophers. His date is uncertain; many scholars assign him to the eighth or early ninth century.

† I Corinthians 3:16.

‡ The elevated state of consciousness in which there is direct experience of God. The conscious state is awareness of the body and

identified with God, you have no karma. This is why the saints say, "Pray unceasingly." When you continuously pray and meditate, you go into the land of superconsciousness, where no troubles can reach you.

❖ ❖ ❖

You can be free from karma right now, by these methods. Whenever karmic troubles plague you, go to sleep. Or, think pure thoughts and make the mind like steel, saying to yourself: "I am above it all." Or, best of all, in deep meditation go into the divine state of superconsciousness. The bliss of that consciousness is the natural state of your soul, but you have forgotten your real nature by being so long identified with the body. That untroubled, blissful state of the soul has to be reacquired.

❖ ❖ ❖

The soul's nature [as individualized Spirit] is bliss: a lasting, inner state of ever-new, ever-changing joy. This bliss eternally gives unfading joy to one who attains it, even when he is passing through trials of physical suffering or death.

❖ ❖ ❖

Material remedies—medicines, physical comforts, human consolation—have their place in

---

its external environment. The subconscious state is the inner mind, operative in sleep and such mental processes as memory. The superconscious state is the transcendent higher mind or spiritual consciousness of the soul. See *samadhi* in glossary.

helping to remove pain, but the greatest remedy is the practice of *Kriya Yoga** and the affirmation that you are one with God. This is the cure-all for every trouble, pain, and bereavement—the way to freedom from all individual and mass karma.†

Affirmations

I know that God's power is limitless; and as I am made in His image, I, too, have the strength to overcome all obstacles.

❖ ❖ ❖

Dear Father, whatever conditions confront me, I know that they represent the next step in my unfoldment. I will welcome all tests because I know that within me is the intelligence to understand and the power to overcome.

---

* A scientific technique of interiorized God-communion. The science of *Kriya Yoga* is explained in Paramahansa Yogananda's *Autobiography of a Yogi*. See glossary.

† The cumulative actions of human beings within communities, nations, or the world as a whole constitute mass karma, which produces local or far-ranging effects according to the degree and preponderance of good or evil. The thoughts and actions of every individual, therefore, contribute to the good or ill of this world and all peoples in it.

CHAPTER 3

Learn to Meditate

Meditation: The Most Practical Science

Meditation is the science of God-realization.* It is the most practical science in the world. Most people would want to meditate if they understood its value and experienced its beneficial effects. The ultimate object of meditation is to attain conscious awareness of God, and of the soul's eternal oneness with Him. What achievement could be more purposeful and useful than to harness limited human faculties to the omnipresence and omnipotence of the Creator? God-realization bestows on the meditator the blessings of the Lord's peace, love, joy, power, and wisdom.

❖ ❖ ❖

Meditation utilizes concentration in its highest form. Concentration consists in freeing the attention from distractions and in focusing it on any thought in which one may be interested. Meditation is that special form of concentration in which the attention

---

* An introductory form of meditation as taught by Paramahansa Yogananda is given in this chapter. The comprehensive set of techniques he gave—the step-by-step *Kriya Yoga* science of concentration and meditation—is given in his printed *Self-Realization Fellowship Lessons*. See page 219.

has been liberated from restlessness and is focused on God. Meditation, therefore, is concentration used to know God.

Preparatory Instructions

Sit on a straight chair, or in a cross-legged position on a firm surface. Keep the spine straight and the chin parallel to the floor.

❖ ❖ ❖

If you have assumed the correct posture, your body will be stable, yet relaxed, so that it is possible to remain completely still, without moving a muscle. Such stillness, devoid of restless body movements and adjustments, is essential to the attainment of a deep meditative state.

❖ ❖ ❖

With the eyelids half closed (or completely closed, if this is more comfortable to you), look upward, focusing the gaze and the attention as though looking out through a point between the eyebrows. (A person deep in concentration often "knits" his brows at this spot.)

Do not cross the eyes or strain them; the upward gaze comes naturally when one is relaxed and calmly concentrated. What *is* important is fixing the *whole attention* at the point between the eyebrows.

This is the Christ Consciousness center, the seat of the single eye spoken of by Christ: "The light of the body is the eye: if therefore thine eye be single, thy whole body shall be full of light" (Matthew 6:22).

When the purpose of meditation is fulfilled, the devotee finds his consciousness automatically concentrated at the spiritual eye, and he experiences, according to his inner spiritual capacity, a state of joyous divine union with Spirit.

A Preliminary Breathing Exercise

When you are established in the meditation pose just described, the next preparation for meditation is to rid the lungs of accumulated carbon dioxide, which causes restlessness.

Expel the breath through the mouth in a double exhalation: "huh, huhhh." (This sound is made with the breath only, not the voice.)

Then inhale deeply through the nostrils and tense the whole body to a count of six.

Expel the breath through the mouth in a double exhalation, "huh, huhhh" and relax the tension.

Repeat this three times.

❖ ❖ ❖

As a first step toward entering the kingdom of God, the devotee should sit still in the correct meditation posture, with erect spine, and tense and relax the body—for by relaxation the consciousness is released from the muscles.

The yogi begins with proper deep breathing, inhaling and tensing the whole body, exhaling and relaxing, several times. With each exhalation all muscular tension and motion should be cast away, until a state of bodily stillness is attained.

Then, by concentration techniques, restless motion is removed from the mind. In perfect stillness of body and mind, the yogi enjoys the ineffable peace of the presence of the soul.

In the body, life is templed; in the mind, light is templed; in the soul, peace is templed. The deeper one goes into the soul the more that peace is felt; that is superconsciousness. When by deeper meditation the devotee expands that awareness of peace and feels his consciousness spreading with it over the universe, that all beings and all creation are swallowed up in that peace, then he is entering into Cosmic Consciousness. He feels that peace everywhere—in the flowers, in every human being, in the atmosphere. He beholds the earth and all worlds floating like bubbles in that ocean of peace.

The inner peace first experienced by the devotee in meditation is his own soul; the vaster peace he feels by going deeper is God. The devotee who experiences unity with everything has established God in the temple of his infinite inner perception.

Concentrate on the Peace and Joy of the Soul

Remain calm....Bid adieu to the world of sensations—sight, hearing, smell, taste, and touch—and go within, where our soul expresses itself....

Dismiss all sensations of the body; dismiss all restless thoughts. Concentrate on the thought of peace and joy.

❖ ❖ ❖

The door to the kingdom of heaven is in the subtle center of transcendent consciousness at the point between the two eyebrows. If you focus your attention on that seat of concentration, you will find tremendous spiritual strength and help from within. Feel that your consciousness is expanding in divine consciousness. Feel that there are no barriers, no attachments to the body, but that you are moving on and on into the kingdom of God, which can be entered through the spiritual eye.*

Pray with me: "Heavenly Father, open my spiritual eye so that I can enter into Thy kingdom of omnipresence. Father, do not leave me behind in this mortal world of misery; lead me from darkness to light, from death to immortality, from ignorance to endless wisdom, from sorrow to eternal joy."

---

* The single eye of intuition and omnipresent perception at the Christ (*Kutastha*) center (*ajna chakra*) between the eyebrows. The spiritual eye is the entryway into the ultimate states of divine consciousness. By awakening and penetrating the spiritual eye, the devotee experiences successively higher states: superconsciousness, Christ Consciousness, and Cosmic Consciousness. The methods of doing so are part of the Kriya Yoga science of meditation, the specific techniques of which are taught to students of Paramahansa Yogananda's *Self-Realization Fellowship Lessons.*

The Deeper Yoga Science of Meditation

Raja Yoga, the royal way of God-union, is the science of actual realization of the kingdom of God that lies within oneself. Through practice of the sacred yoga techniques of interiorization received during initiation from a true guru, one can find that kingdom by awakening the astral and causal centers of life force and consciousness in the spine and brain that are the gateways into the heavenly regions of transcendent consciousness.*

❖ ❖ ❖

Prayer alone will not do. People wonder why they pray so hard and still do not get a personal response from God. They do not know how to meditate. That is why yoga is necessary. If you practice the Self-Realization yoga techniques, you will get there. Yoga does not tell you merely to believe and you will be saved; it teaches you the scientific laws and techniques by which you can feel God in your own consciousness. It is only when you actually commune with God that He will respond openly. Not before. He can't. When your consciousness is closed behind the door of your ignorance, God cannot enter in. When you will open that door, God will reveal Himself; and in that realization all things become possible. However, you have to make the effort. You won't find God if you sit for meditation and your mind roams about on different

---

* See *Raja Yoga, Kriya Yoga,* and *chakras* in glossary.

subjects. But if you practice the techniques regularly, you will find Him.

A Guided Meditation Exercise

Let us meditate.

Feel that you are charged with the creative, life-sustaining energy of God.

Feel that the everlasting consciousness of God is manifesting in your body, erasing the mortal consciousness of past failures, fear, disease, old age.

Repeat this thought with deep attention:

"Father, Thou art present in my body, in my mind, in my soul. I am made in Thine image. Bless my body, mind, and soul, that they shine with Thine everlasting youth, power, immortality, and joy.

Aum. Peace. Amen."

A Meditation on Peace

Mentally call to God with all the fervor and sincerity of your hearts. Consciously invoke Him in the temple of silence; and in deeper meditation, find Him in the temple of ecstasy and bliss. Through your thoughts and feelings, send Him your love with all your heart, mind, soul, and strength. Through the intuition of your soul feel the manifestation of God bursting through the clouds of your restlessness as great peace and joy. Peace and joy are the voices of God that have long slumbered beneath your ignorance, ignored and forgotten in the din of human passions.

The kingdom of God is just behind the darkness of closed eyes, and the first gate that opens to it is your peace. Exhale and relax, and feel this peace spread everywhere, within and without. Immerse yourself in that peace.

Inhale deeply. Exhale. Now forget your breath. Repeat after me:

Father, hushed are the sounds of the world and the heavens.

I am in the temple of quietness.

Thine eternal kingdom of peace is spread tier upon tier before my gaze. May this infinite kingdom, long hidden behind the darkness, remain manifest within me.

Peace fills my body; peace fills my heart and dwells within my love; peace within, without, everywhere.

God is peace. I am His child. I am peace. God and I are one.

Infinite peace surrounds my life and permeates all the moments of my existence. Peace unto myself; peace unto my family; peace unto my nation; peace unto my world; peace unto my cosmos.

Goodwill to all nations, goodwill to all creatures; for all are my brothers and God is our common Father. We live in the United States of the World with God and Truth as our leaders.

Heavenly Father, may Thy kingdom of peace come on earth as it is in heaven, that we all be freed from divisive inharmonies and become perfect citizens, in body, mind, and soul, of Thy world.

Meditate Until You Feel Divine Response

You should continue to concentrate at the Christ Consciousness center between the eyebrows, praying deeply to God and His great saints. In the language of your heart invoke their presence and their blessings. A good practice is to take an affirmation or a prayer...and spiritualize it with your own devotional yearning. Silently chant and pray to God, keeping the attention at the point between the eyebrows, until you feel God's response as calm, deep peace and inner joy.

❖ ❖ ❖

When by consistent practice your meditation begins to deepen, you may see a little light or hear the astral sounds or see a vision of some saint. At first you tend to discount it as only hallucination; but as you go on with yearning and devotion, applying the law, you see that wonderful things begin to happen in your life in mysterious ways....

God is responsive to you; He will sustain and guide you in everything—in the selection of your friends or business partners or in everyday decisions—when you will be in tune with Him.

CHAPTER 4

Rising Above Suffering

I have had continual controversy with my Heavenly Father as to why pain is a test to bring back to Him human beings who are made in His image. I tell the Father that in pain there is a compulsion; persuasion and love are better ways to get human beings back to heaven. Even though I know the answer, I have always fought with God on these points, for He understands me as a father understands his son.

❖ ❖ ❖

How tragic is this world! It is a place of uncertainty. But no matter what has happened to you, if you throw yourself at the feet of the Father and seek His mercy, He will lift you up and show you that life is but a dream.*

❖ ❖ ❖

I will tell you a little story. A king fell asleep and dreamed that he was poor. He was crying out in his sleep for just a penny for some food. Finally, the queen woke him and said, "What is the matter with you? Your treasury is full of gold, and yet you are crying for a penny."

Then the king said, "Oh, how silly of me. I thought I was a beggar and was starving for lack of that penny."

* See *maya* in glossary.

Such is the delusion of every soul who is dreaming he is a mortal, subject to the nightmarish evils of all kinds of disease, suffering, troubles, heartbreaks. The only way to escape this nightmare is by becoming more attached to God and less attached to the dream images of this world.

❖ ❖ ❖

No cruelty exists in God's plan, because in His eyes there is no good or evil—only pictures of light and shadows. The Lord intended us to view the dualistic scenes of life as He does Himself—the ever joyous Witness of a stupendous cosmic drama.

Man has falsely identified himself with the pseudo-soul or ego. When he transfers his sense of identity to his true being, the immortal soul, he discovers that all pain is unreal. He no longer can even *imagine* the state of suffering.

❖ ❖ ❖

The superconsciousness of man is made of God and is painproof. All physical and mental sufferings come by identification, imagination, and wrong human habits of thinking.

❖ ❖ ❖

Have more mental strength. Develop such mental power that you can stand unshaken, no matter what comes, bravely facing anything in life. If you love God you should have faith and be prepared to endure when trials come. Don't be afraid of suffering.

Keep your mind positive and strong. It is your inner experience that is most important.

❖ ❖ ❖

You heighten suffering by imagination. Worrying or feeling sorry for yourself won't ease your pain, but rather increase it. For instance, someone wrongs you; you dwell on it, and your friends talk about it and sympathize with you. The more you think of it, the more you magnify the hurt—*and* your suffering.

❖ ❖ ❖

Some people go on remembering all the suffering they passed through, and how terrible the pain was, from an operation that took place twenty years ago! Over and over again they relive the consciousness of that sickness. Why repeat such experiences?

❖ ❖ ❖

The best way to dissociate yourself from your difficulty is to be mentally detached, as if you were merely a spectator, while at the same time seeking a remedy.*

❖ ❖ ❖

The fact is, if you learn to live in your body without thinking of it as yourself, you won't suffer so much. The connection between you and bodily pain is only mental. When you are asleep and unconscious

* Persons with serious or persistent health problems—pain or other symptoms—should follow the advice of a medical doctor.

of the body, you feel no pain. Likewise, when a doctor or a dentist gives you an anesthetic and performs surgery on your body, you don't feel any pain. The mind has been disconnected from the sensation.

❖ ❖ ❖

Look after the body, but be above it. Know that you are separate from your mortal form. Put up a great mental barrier between your mind and body. Affirm: "I am apart from the body. No heat, cold, or sickness can touch me. I am free." Your limitations will become less and less.

❖ ❖ ❖

The best anesthesia against pain is your mental power. If your mind refuses to accept it, pain will be greatly lessened. I have seen, at times when this body got hurt and felt severe pain, that if I put my mind at the Christ center* —that is, if I identify myself more with God and less with the body—there is no pain at all. So when pain comes, concentrate at the Christ center. Be mentally apart from pain; develop more strength of mind. Be tough within. When you are feeling pain, inwardly say to yourself, "It doesn't hurt me." When a hurt comes, recognize

---

* The seat of the singular eye of divine consciousness and spiritual perception at the point between the eyebrows, of which Jesus spoke when he said: "If therefore thine eye be single, thy whole body shall be full of light" (Matthew 6:22). Pictures of saints in divine communion often show them with their eyes thus upturned to this center. See glossary.

it as something to be cared for, but don't suffer over it. The more you concentrate on the power of the mind, the more your body consciousness drops away.

❖ ❖ ❖

"Pain and pleasure are transitory," [Sri Yukteswar* told his disciples]. "Endure all dualities with calmness, trying at the same time to remove yourself beyond their power."

❖ ❖ ❖

In the midst of negative conditions, practice "opposition" by thinking and acting in a positive, constructive way. Practice *titiksha*,† which means not to give in to unpleasant experiences, but to resist them without becoming upset mentally. When sickness comes, follow hygienic laws of living, without permitting your mind to be disturbed. Be unruffled in everything you do.

❖ ❖ ❖

Whether you are suffering in this life, or smiling with opulence and power, your consciousness should remain unchanged. If you can accomplish evenmindedness, nothing can ever hurt you. The lives of all great masters show that they have achieved this blessed state.

❖ ❖ ❖

* Swami Sri Yukteswar (1855–1936) was the guru (spiritual preceptor) of Paramahansa Yogananda. His life is described in the latter's *Autobiography of a Yogi.* See glossary.

† Sanskrit, "endurance with mental evenness."

Meditation is the way by which you must strive to rise above delusion and know your true nature. If you can hold on to that consciousness in activity as well as in meditation, remaining undisturbed by delusive experiences, then you will be above this dream world of God's. The dream will be over for you. This is why Lord Krishna* stressed that if you want freedom in Spirit, you must be of even mind under all circumstances: "He who cannot be ruffled by these (contacts of the senses with their objects), who is calm and evenminded during pain and pleasure, he alone is fit to attain everlastingness!"†

❖ ❖ ❖

When tigers of worries, sickness, and death are chasing you, your only sanctuary is the inner temple of silence. The spiritually deep man lives day and night in a calm interior silence into which neither menacing worries nor even the crash of colliding worlds can intrude.

❖ ❖ ❖

No sensation or mental torture can affect you if the mind is dissociated from it and anchored in the peace and joy of God.

---

* An avatar (divine incarnation) who lived in ancient India ages before the Christian era. Lord Krishna's discourse to the disciple Arjuna on the battlefield of Kurukshetra forms the immortal scripture, *Bhagavad Gita*. See *Bhagavan Krishna* and *Bhagavad Gita* in glossary.

† Bhagavad Gita II:15.

The Healing Power of God

There are two ways in which our needs can be taken care of. One is the material. For example, when we have ill health we can go to a doctor for medical treatment. But a time comes when no human aid can help. Then we look to the other way, to the Spiritual Power, the Maker of our body, mind, and soul. Material power is limited, and when it fails, we turn to the unlimited Divine Power. Likewise with our financial needs; when we have done our best, and still it is inadequate, we turn to that other Power.

❖ ❖ ❖

To know God is the most important way to heal all disease—physical, mental, spiritual. As darkness cannot remain where light is, so also the darkness of disease is driven away by the light of God's perfect presence when it enters the body.

❖ ❖ ❖

The unlimited power of God is working behind all methods of healing, whether physical, mental, or vital.* This fact must never be forgotten, for if one depends upon the *method* and not upon *God*, he automatically hinders and limits the free flow of the healing power.

❖ ❖ ❖

* "Vital" healing refers to tapping the cosmic energy—the intelligent, finer-than-atomic energy—that is the universal life-principle through which God sustains all creation. See *prana* in glossary.

Your duty is to bring your need to God's attention, and to do your part in helping God to bring that desire to fruition. For example, in chronic diseases, do your best to help promote healing, but know in your mind that ultimately God alone can help.

❖ ❖ ❖

An unlimited source of protection for man lies in his strong thought that, as a child of God, he cannot be affected by disease.

❖ ❖ ❖

Do your best to remove the causes of illness and then be absolutely unafraid. There are so many germs everywhere that if you began to fear them you would not be able to enjoy life at all....Be fearless.

❖ ❖ ❖

Keep smiling within, pulsating with deep joy, ever ready to act, and spiritually ambitious to help others. These attitudes are not only good exercises for the mind; they also keep the body constantly supplied with fresh cosmic energy.

❖ ❖ ❖

He who finds joy within himself discovers that his body is charged with electric current, life energy, not from food but from God. If you feel that you can't smile, stand before a mirror and with your fingers pull your mouth into a smile. It is that important!...

When one is joyful within, he invites the help of the inexhaustible power of God. I mean a sincere joyfulness, not that which you feign outwardly but do not feel within. When your joy is sincere you are a smile-millionaire. A genuine smile distributes the cosmic current, *prana*, to every body cell. The happy man is less subject to disease, for happiness actually attracts into the body a greater supply of the universal life energy.

❖ ❖ ❖

In the vault of the mind lie all the chains of bondage, as well as the keys to freedom.

❖ ❖ ❖

Mind power carries with it the unfailing energy of God; that is the power you want in your body. And there is a way to bring in that power. The way is communion with God by meditation. When your communion with Him is perfect, the healing is permanent.

The Power of Affirmation and Prayer

In the past you may have been disappointed that your prayers were not answered. But do not lose faith....God is not a mute unfeeling Being. He is love itself. If you know how to meditate to make contact with Him, He will respond to your loving demands.

❖ ❖ ❖

To know exactly how and when to pray, according to the nature of our needs, is what brings the desired results. When the right method is applied, it sets in motion the proper laws of God; the operation of these laws scientifically bears results.

❖ ❖ ❖

The first rule in prayer is to approach God only with legitimate desires. The second is to pray for their fulfillment, not as a beggar, but as a son: "I am Thy child. Thou art my Father. Thou and I are One." When you pray deeply and continuously you will feel a great joy welling up in your heart. Don't be satisfied until that joy manifests; for when you feel that all-satisfying joy in your heart, you will know that God has tuned in your prayer broadcast. Then pray to your Father: "Lord, this is my need. I am willing to work for it; please guide me and help me to have the right thoughts and to do the right things to bring about success. I will use my reason, and work with determination, but guide Thou my reason, will, and activity to the right thing that I should do."

❖ ❖ ❖

You should pray to God intimately, as His child, which you are. God does not object when you pray from your ego, as a stranger and a beggar, but you will find that your efforts are limited by that consciousness. God does not want you to give up your own will power, which is your divine birthright as His child.

❖ ❖ ❖

An unceasing demand* for anything, mentally whispered with unflagging zeal and unflinching courage and faith, develops into a dynamic power that so influences the entire behavior of the conscious, subconscious, and superconscious powers of man that the desired object is gained. The inner performance of mental whispers must be unceasing, undaunted by reverses. Then the desired-for object will materialize.

Technique of Affirmation

The infinite potencies of sound derive from the Creative Word, *Aum,†* the cosmic vibratory power behind all atomic energies. Any word spoken with clear realization and deep concentration has a materializing value.

❖ ❖ ❖

Words saturated with sincerity, conviction, faith, and intuition are like highly explosive vibration bombs, which, when set off, shatter the rocks of difficulties and create the change desired.

❖ ❖ ❖

* Paramahansa Yogananda taught: "Prayer often implies the consciousness of beggary. We are children of God, not beggars, and are thus entitled to our divine inheritance. When we have established a connection of love between our souls and God, we have a right to lovingly *demand* the fulfillment of our legitimate prayers." This principle of demanding our birthright from God is the enlivening power within an affirmation.

† The great Amen or "Word of God." See *Aum* in glossary.

The subconscious idea-habit of disease or health exerts a strong influence. Stubborn mental or physical diseases always have a deep root in the subconsciousness. Illness may be cured by pulling out its hidden roots. That is why all affirmations of the conscious mind should be *impressive* enough to permeate the subconsciousness, which in turn automatically influences the conscious mind. Strong conscious affirmations thus react on the mind and body through the medium of the subconsciousness. Still stronger affirmations reach not only the subconscious but also the superconscious mind—the magic storehouse of miraculous powers.

❖ ❖ ❖

Patience and attentive, intelligent repetition are wonder-workers. Affirmations for curing chronic mental or bodily afflictions should be repeated often,* deeply and continuously (utterly ignoring unchanged or contrary conditions, if any), until they become part of one's profound intuitional convictions.

❖ ❖ ❖

Choose your affirmation and repeat all of it, first loudly, then softly and more slowly, until your voice becomes a whisper. Then gradually affirm it

---

* Affirmations for specific purposes are given at the end of each chapter in this book. In *Scientific Healing Affirmations, Metaphysical Meditations,* and *Self-Realization Lessons,* Paramahansa Yogananda provides hundreds of other affirmations for healing, self-improvement, and deepening one's awareness of God.

mentally only, without moving the tongue or the lips, until you feel that you have attained deep, unbroken concentration—not unconsciousness, but a profound continuity of uninterrupted thought.

If you continue with your mental affirmation, and go still deeper, you will feel a sense of increasing joy and peace. During the state of deep concentration, your affirmation will merge with the subconscious stream, to come back later reinforced with power to influence your conscious mind through the law of habit.

During the time that you experience ever-increasing peace, your affirmation goes deeper, into the superconscious realm, to return later laden with unlimited power to influence your conscious mind and also to fulfill your desires. Doubt not and you shall witness the miracle of this scientific faith.

❖ ❖ ❖

Blind repetition of demands or affirmations, without concomitant devotion or spontaneous love, makes one merely a "praying victrola," which does not know what its prayer means. Grinding out prayers vocally and mechanically, while inwardly thinking of something else, does not bring response from God. A blind repetition, taking the name of God in vain, is fruitless. Repeating a demand or prayer over and over again, mentally or orally, and with deepening attention and devotion, spiritualizes the prayer, and changes conscious, believing repetition into superconscious experience.

❖ ❖ ❖

Meditate on the meaning of the demand you have selected, until it becomes a part of you. Saturate the demand with devotion as you meditate upon it. As your meditation becomes deeper, increase your devotion and mentally offer the demand as your own heart's outburst. Imbue yourself with faith that your heart's craving, expressed through this specific demand, is being felt by God.

Feel that just behind the screen of your devotional demand God is listening to the silent words of your soul. Feel this! Be one with your heart's demand—and be thoroughly convinced that He has listened to you. Then go about your duties, seeking not to know whether God will grant your demand. Believe absolutely that your demand has been heard, and that you will know that what is God's is yours also. Unceasingly meditate on God; and when you feel Him, you will acquire your rightful inheritance as His divine son.

❖ ❖ ❖

"The Lord responds to all and works for all," [Sri Yukteswar said]. "Seldom do men realize how often God heeds their prayers. He is not partial to a few, but listens to everyone who approaches Him trustfully. His children should ever have implicit faith in the loving-kindness of their Omnipresent Father."

❖ ❖ ❖

Faith has to be cultivated, or rather uncovered

within us. It is there but has to be brought out. If you watch your life you will see the innumerable ways in which God works through it; your faith will thus be strengthened. Few people look for His hidden hand. Most men consider the course of events as natural and inevitable. They little know what radical changes are possible through prayer!

Cultivating Faith in God

Absolute, unquestioning faith in God is the greatest method of instantaneous healing. An unceasing effort to arouse that faith is man's highest and most rewarding duty.

❖ ❖ ❖

Belief in God and faith in God are different. A belief is valueless if you don't test it and live by it. Belief converted into experience becomes faith.

❖ ❖ ❖

You may want to believe; you may even think you believe; but if you really believe, the result will be instantaneous.

❖ ❖ ❖

Faith cannot be contradicted: it is intuitive conviction of truth, and it cannot be shaken even by contrary evidence....You don't realize how wonderfully this great power works. It operates mathematically.

There is no "if" about it. And that is what the Bible means by faith: it is *proof* of things unseen.[*]

❖ ❖ ❖

Always undoubtingly believe that God's power is working in you, just behind your thoughts, prayers, and convictions, to give infinite strength....Acknowledge His working within you in everything and you will have Him always with you.

❖ ❖ ❖

The Supreme Power may be invoked by continuous faith and unceasing prayer. You should eat rightly and do whatever else is necessary for the body, but continuously pray to Him: "Lord, Thou canst heal me because Thou dost control the life atoms and subtle conditions of the body that doctors cannot reach with medicines."

❖ ❖ ❖

In a voice resounding with joy, [Lahiri Mahasaya[†] said]: "Always know that the omnipotent Paramatman[‡] can heal anyone, doctor or no doctor."

❖ ❖ ❖

This is God's world. He takes you; He keeps you. When the doctor says, "Well, I'll heal you," if God

---

[*] "Faith is the substance of things hoped for, the evidence of things not seen" (Hebrews 11:1).

[†] The guru of Paramahansa Yogananda's guru. See glossary.

[‡] Sanskrit, "Supreme Spirit."

makes up His mind to take you, you will go. So live your life for Him.

❖ ❖ ❖

An ill person should try earnestly to rid himself of his malady. Then, even if doctors proclaim there is no hope, he should remain tranquil, for fear shuts the eyes of faith to the omnipotent, compassionate Divine Presence. Instead of indulging anxiety he should affirm: "I am ever safe in the fortress of Thy loving care." A fearless devotee, succumbing to an incurable disease, concentrates on the Lord and becomes ready for liberation from the bodily prison into a glorious afterlife in the astral world. Thereby he advances closer to the goal of supreme liberation in his next life....All men are meant to realize that soul consciousness can triumph over every external disaster.

❖ ❖ ❖

Even death is nothing to the spiritually strong. I once dreamed I was dying. Nevertheless I was praying to Him: "Lord, it is all right; whatever is Thy will." Then He touched me and I realized the truth: "How can I die? The wave cannot die; it sinks back into the ocean and comes forth again. The wave never dies; and I can never die."

❖ ❖ ❖

[During a period of great trial, Paramahansa Yogananda retired to the desert for solitude and prayer. One night

while deeply meditating, he received this beautiful response from God:]

"Dance of life or dance of death,
Know that these come from Me, and rejoice.
What more dost thou want, than that thou
hast Me?"

❖ ❖ ❖

[*The exemplary lives of saintly souls are inexhaustible sources of strength and inspiration to others. The right attitude toward suffering found perfect expression in the life of Sri Gyanamata (1869–1951),* one of the foremost disciples of Paramahansa Yogananda. All who knew her were uplifted by her quiet heroism, her inner strength and love for God that never wavered despite the great physical suffering she endured for the last two decades of her life. During the memorial service for her conducted by Paramahansaji, he spoke these words:*]

Sister's life has been like that of St. Francis, who suffered even while helping others. So she stands as a great inspiration. In all those years she suffered, she showed that her love for God was greater; and I never saw one mark of that suffering in her eyes. That is why she is a great saint—a great soul—and that is why she is with God....

When I looked at her body in the casket, I felt Sister's soul commingled with the omnipresent ether, and I heard the voice of the Father speaking

---

* Gyanamata means "Mother of Wisdom." Her wise and loving counsel and encouragement to others are beautifully expressed in the collection of her letters and account of her life in *God Alone,* published by Self-Realization Fellowship.

to me from within: "Twenty years of suffering never took away her love from Me, and that is what I prize in her life." I could not say anything more; I realized that the Heavenly Father has a right to test our love for Him with pain, for even twenty years or more, in order that we may claim in exchange our lost eternal, ever new happiness as His image.

Then again I choked with the thrill of God's presence, and I said to myself: "To regain the eternity of ever new joy through twenty years of being unruffled by pain is the greater achievement, through the grace of the Father."

❖ ❖ ❖

If you live with the Lord, you will be healed of the delusions of life and death, health and sickness. Be in the Lord. Feel His love. Fear nothing. Only in the castle of God can we find protection. There is no safer haven of joy than in His presence. When you are with Him, nothing can touch you.

Affirmations for Healing

God's perfect health permeates the dark nooks of my bodily sickness. In all my cells His healing light is shining. They are entirely well, for His perfection is in them.

❖ ❖ ❖

The healing power of Spirit is flowing through

all the cells of my body. I am made of the one
universal God-substance.

❖ ❖ ❖

Thy perfect light is omnipresent in all my body
parts. Wherever that healing light is manifest,
there is perfection. I am well, for perfection is
in me.

❖ ❖ ❖

I am castled in God's presence. No harm can
reach me, for in every situation of life—physical, mental, financial, spiritual—I am protected in the fortress of God's presence.

CHAPTER 5

Security in an Uncertain World

The sudden cataclysms that occur in nature, creating havoc and mass injury, are not "acts of God." Such disasters result from the thoughts and actions of man. Whenever the world's vibratory balance of good and evil is disturbed by an accumulation of harmful vibrations, the result of man's wrong thinking and wrong doing, you will see devastation....*

Wars are brought about not by fateful divine action but by widespread material selfishness. Banish selfishness — individual, industrial, political, national — and you will have no more wars.

❖ ❖ ❖

Modern chaotic conditions all over the world are the result of living by ungodly ideals. Individuals and nations can be protected from utter destruction if they live by heavenly ideals of brotherhood, industrial cooperation, and international exchange of earthly goods and experiences.

❖ ❖ ❖

I believe a time will come when in greater understanding we shall have no boundaries anymore.

---

* See footnote on page 20.

We shall call the earth our country; and we shall, by a process of justice and international assembly, distribute unselfishly the goods of the world according to the needs of the people. But equality cannot be established by force; it must come from the heart.... We must start now, with ourselves. We should try to be like the divine ones who have come on earth again and again to show us the way. By our loving each other and keeping our understanding clear, as they taught and exemplified, peace can come.

❖ ❖ ❖

You may think it is hopeless to try to conquer hatred and inspire mankind to Christlike ways of love, but never was the need so great as now. Atheistic ideologies are battling to drive religion out. The world is marching on in a wild drama of existence. Trying to stop the raging storms, we seem no more than little ants swimming in the ocean. But do not minimize your power.

❖ ❖ ❖

The one thing that will help to eliminate world suffering—more than money, houses, or any other material aid—is to meditate and transmit to others the divine consciousness of God that we feel. A thousand dictators could never destroy what I have within. Every day radiate His consciousness to others. Try to understand God's plan for mankind—to draw all souls back to Himself—and work in harmony with His will.

❖ ❖ ❖

God is Love; His plan for creation can be rooted only in love. Does not that simple thought, rather than erudite reasonings, offer solace to the human heart? Every saint who has penetrated to the core of Reality has testified that a divine universal plan exists and that it is beautiful and full of joy.

❖ ❖ ❖

As soon as we learn in meditation to love God, we shall love all mankind as we love our own family. Those who have found God through their own Self-realization—those who have actually experienced God—they alone *can* love mankind; not impersonally, but as their blood brothers, children of the same one Father.

❖ ❖ ❖

Realize that the same lifeblood is circulating in the veins of all races. How may anyone dare to hate any other human being, of whatever race, when God lives and breathes in all? We are Americans or Hindus or other nationalities for just a few years, but we are God's children forever. The soul cannot be confined within man-made boundaries. Its nationality is Spirit; its country is Omnipresence.

❖ ❖ ❖

If you contact God within yourself, you will know that He is in everyone, that He has become the children of all races. Then you cannot be an enemy to anyone. If the whole world could love with that universal love, there would be no need for men to arm themselves against one another. By our own Christlike example we must bring unity among all religions, all nations, all races.

❖ ❖ ❖

The broad sympathies and discerning insight needed for the healing of earthly woes cannot flow from a mere intellectual consideration of human diversities, but from knowledge of men's deepest unity — kinship with God. Toward realization of the world's highest ideal — peace through brotherhood — may Yoga, the science of personal communion with the Divine, spread in time to all men in all lands.

❖ ❖ ❖

The grim march of world political events points inexorably to the truth that without spiritual vision, the people perish. Science, if not religion, has awakened in humanity a dim sense of the insecurity and even insubstantiality of all material things. Where indeed may man go now, if not to his Source and Origin, the Spirit within him?

❖ ❖ ❖

The Atomic Age will see men's minds sobered and broadened by the now scientifically indisputable truth that matter is in reality a concentrate of energy. The human mind can and must liberate within itself energies greater than those within stones and metals, lest the material atomic giant, newly unleashed, turn on the world in mindless destruction. An indirect benefit of mankind's concern over atomic bombs may be an increased practical interest in the science of Yoga, a "bombproof shelter" truly.

❖ ❖ ❖

This world will always have turmoil and trouble. What are you worried about? Go to the shelter of God, where the Masters have gone, and whence they are watching and helping the world. You shall have safety forever, not only for yourself, but for all those loved ones who have been entrusted to your care by our Lord and Father.

❖ ❖ ❖

True happiness, lasting happiness, lies only in God, "having whom no other gain is greater."* In Him is the only safety, the only shelter, the only escape from all our fears. You have no other security in the world, no other freedom. The only true freedom lies in God. So strive deeply to contact Him in meditation morning and night, as well as throughout the day in all work and duties you perform. Yoga teaches that where God is, there is no fear, no sorrow. The successful yogi† can stand unshaken midst the crash of breaking worlds; he is secure in the realization: "Lord, where I am, there Thou must come."

❖ ❖ ❖

Don't be attached to the passing dreams of life.

---

* Paraphrase of Bhagavad Gita VI:22.
† See glossary.

Live for God and God alone. This is the only way to
have freedom and safety in this world. Outside of
God there is no security; no matter where you go,
delusion can attack you. Be free right now. Be a son of
God now; realize you are His child, so that you may
be rid of this dream of delusion forever.* Meditate
deeply and faithfully, and one day you will wake up
in ecstasy with God and see how foolish it is that
people think they are suffering. You and I and they
are all pure Spirit.

❖ ❖ ❖

Be not afraid of the frightening dream of this
world. Awaken in God's immortal light! There was
a time when life, to me, was like helplessly watching a terrifying movie, and I was giving too much
importance to the tragedies being enacted therein.
Then, one day while I was meditating, a great light
appeared in my room and God's voice said to me:
"What are you dreaming about? Behold My eternal
light, in which the many nightmares of the world
come and go. They are not real." What a tremendous
consolation it was! Nightmares, however dreadful,
are merely nightmares. Movies, whether enjoyable
or disturbing, are merely movies. We ought not to
keep our minds so absorbed in the sad and frightening dramas of this life. Is it not wiser to place our
attention on that Power which is indestructible and
unchanging? Why worry about the unpleasant sur-
prises in the plot of this world movie! We are here

* See *maya* in glossary.

for just a little while. Learn the lesson of the drama of life and find your freedom.

❖ ❖ ❖

Just beneath the shadows of this life is God's wondrous Light. The universe is a vast temple of His presence. When you meditate, you will find doors opening to Him everywhere. When you have communion with Him, not all the ravages of the world can take away that Joy and Peace.

Affirmation

In life and death, in disease, famine, pestilence, or poverty may I ever cling to Thee. Help me to realize I am immortal Spirit, untouched by the changes of childhood, youth, age, and world upheavals.

CHAPTER 6

Wisdom to Solve Problems and Make Life's Decisions

The world will go on like this in its ups and downs. Where shall we look for a sense of direction? Not to the prejudices roused within us by our habits and the environmental influences of our families, our country, or the world; but to the guiding voice of Truth within.

❖ ❖ ❖

Truth is no theory, no speculative system of philosophy, no intellectual insight. Truth is exact correspondence with Reality. For man, truth is unshakable knowledge of his real nature, his Self as soul.

❖ ❖ ❖

In everyday living, truth is a consciousness that is guided by spiritual wisdom, which propels us to do certain things, not because anybody says to, but because they are right.

❖ ❖ ❖

When you are in direct contact with the Creator of this universe, you are in direct contact with all wisdom and understanding.

❖ ❖ ❖

It is not a pumping-in from the outside that gives wisdom; it is the power and extent of your inner receptivity that determines how much you can attain of true knowledge, and how rapidly.

❖ ❖ ❖

When a problem comes up, instead of dwelling on it, think of every possible avenue of action to rid yourself of it. If you are unable to think, compare your particular trouble with others' similar troubles, and from their experiences learn which ways lead to failure and which ways lead to success. Choose those steps that seem logical and practical, and then get busy implementing them. The whole library of the universe is hidden within you. All the things you want to know are within yourself. To bring them out, think creatively.

❖ ❖ ❖

Perhaps you are seriously concerned about your child, or your health, or a mortgage payment. Not finding an immediate solution, you start worrying about the situation. And what do you get? A headache, nervousness, heart trouble. Because you do not clearly analyze yourself and your problems, you do not know how to control your feelings or the condition that confronts you. Instead of wasting time worrying, think positively about how the cause of the problem can be removed. If you want to get rid of a trouble, calmly analyze your difficulty, setting down point by point the pros and cons of the matter; then determine what steps might be best to accomplish your goal.

❖ ❖ ❖

There is always a way out of your trouble; and if you take the time to think clearly, to think how to get rid of the cause of your anxiety instead of just worrying about it, you become a master.

❖ ❖ ❖

All successful men and women devote much time to deep concentration. They are able to dive deeply within their minds and to find the pearls of right solutions for the problems that confront them. If you learn how to withdraw your attention from all objects of distraction and to place it upon one object of concentration,* you too will know how to attract at will whatever you need.

Developing Discriminative Judgment

When the mind is calm, how quickly, how smoothly, how beautifully you will perceive everything.

❖ ❖ ❖

A calm person reflects restfulness in his eyes, keen intelligence in his face, and proper receptivity in his mind. He is a man of decisive and prompt action, but he is not moved by impulses and desires that suddenly occur to him.

❖ ❖ ❖

* A reference to the scientific yoga techniques of concentration taught in the *Self-Realization Fellowship Lessons.*

Always think first of what you are about to do
and how it will affect you. To act on impulse is not
freedom, for you will be bound by the unpleasant
effects of wrong actions. But to do those things
your discrimination tells you are good for you is all-
freeing. That kind of wisdom-guided action makes
for a divine existence.

❖ ❖ ❖

Man should not be a psychological automaton,
like the animal, which acts only through instinct.
To be unthinking is a great sin against Spirit, which
abides in you; we are meant to be conscious of what
we do. We should reflect before we act. We should
learn how to use our minds so that we can evolve
and realize our oneness with the Creator. Everything
we do should be the result of premeditated thought.

❖ ❖ ❖

A student had made a serious error. She lamented,
"I have always cultivated good habits. It seems incredible that this misfortune should have happened
to me."

"Your mistake was to rely too heavily on good
habits and to neglect constant exercise of right judgment," Paramahansa Yogananda said. "Your good
habits help you in ordinary and familiar situations
but may not suffice to guide you when a new problem arises. Then discrimination is necessary. By
deeper meditation you will learn to choose the right
course in everything, even when confronted by extraordinary circumstances.

"Man is not an automaton, and therefore cannot always live wisely by simply following set rules and rigid moral precepts. In the great variety of daily problems and events, we find scope for the development of good judgment."

❖ ❖ ❖

Restlessness—that which ruffles and diffuses the mind—blurs vision and causes misunderstanding. Emotion blurs your vision. Moods blur your vision. Most people act, not out of understanding, but according to their moods.

❖ ❖ ❖

Understanding is the vision of your inner being, the sight of your soul, the telescope of your heart. Understanding is a balance of calm intelligence and purity of heart....Emotion is distorted feeling that will lead you to do the wrong thing. And understanding that is guided solely by the intellect is cold-blooded; it too will teach you to do wrong.... You must have balanced understanding. If your understanding is governed by both heart and head, then you have clear vision to see yourself and others.

❖ ❖ ❖

You should analyze the many prejudices that your understanding is subject to. Any time you are making a decision or taking action, ask yourself if you are doing it through understanding, or through emotion or some other prejudicial influence on your

mind. As long as you are subject to greed or anger;
as long as you are influenced by the wrong thinking
of others; as long as you are affected by the misunderstanding of others, so long will your own understanding be unclear.

❖ ❖ ❖

Human reason can always find the "pros and
cons" for good and for bad actions alike; it is inher-
ently disloyal. Discrimination acknowledges only
one polestar criterion: the soul.

❖ ❖ ❖

Picture two men. On their right is the valley of
life, and on their left is the valley of death. Both are
men of reason, but one goes right and the other goes
left. Why? Because one has used correctly his power
of discrimination, and the other has misused that
power by indulging in false rationalizations.

❖ ❖ ❖

Watch your motives in everything. Both the
greedy man and the yogi eat. But would you say that
eating is a sin because it is often associated with
greed? No. Sin lies in the thought, in the motive.
The worldly man eats to satisfy his greed, and the
yogi eats to keep his body well. There is a lot of
difference. Similarly, one man commits murder and
is hanged for it; another man kills many human beings on the battlefield in defense of his country and
is given a medal. Again, it is the motive that makes
the difference. Moralists make absolute rules, but

I am giving you illustrations to show you how you can live in this world of relativity with self-control of feeling but without being an automaton.

❖ ❖ ❖

The scientific way to live is to go within yourself and ask yourself whether you are doing right or wrong, and be absolutely sincere with yourself. If you are sincere with yourself, you are unlikely ever to go wrong; and even if you do, you will be able quickly to correct yourself.

❖ ❖ ❖

Every morning and night go into silence or deep meditation, for meditation is the only way to discriminate between truth and error.

❖ ❖ ❖

Learn to be guided by your conscience, the divine discriminative power within you.

❖ ❖ ❖

God is the whisper in the temple of your conscience, and He is the light of intuition. You know when you are doing wrong; your whole being tells you, and that feeling is God's voice. If you don't listen to Him, He becomes quiet. But when you wake up from your delusion, and want to do right, He will guide you.

❖ ❖ ❖

By constantly following the inner voice of

conscience, which is the voice of God, you will become a truly moral person, a highly spiritual being, a man of peace.

Intuition: Insight of the Soul

Intuition is soul guidance, appearing naturally in man during those instants when his mind is calm.... The goal of yoga science is to calm the mind, that without distortion it may hear the infallible counsel of the Inner Voice.

❖ ❖ ❖

"Solve all your problems through meditation," [Lahiri Mahasaya said]. "Attune yourself to the active inner Guidance; the Divine Voice has the answer to every dilemma of life. Though man's ingenuity for getting himself into trouble appears to be endless, the Infinite Succor is no less resourceful."

❖ ❖ ❖

In wanting us to depend on Him alone, God does not mean that you should not think for yourself; He wants you to use your initiative. The idea is, if you fail to seek conscious attunement with God first, you cut off the Source, and so you cannot receive His help. When you look to Him first for all things, He will guide you; He will reveal to you what your mistakes are so that you can change yourself and change the course of your life.

❖ ❖ ❖

Remember, greater than a million reasonings of the mind is to sit and meditate upon God until you feel calmness within. Then say to the Lord, "I can't solve my problem alone, even if I thought a zillion different thoughts; but I can solve it by placing it in Your hands, asking first for Your guidance, and then following through by thinking out the various angles for a possible solution." God does help those who help themselves. When your mind is calm and filled with faith after praying to God in meditation, you are able to see various answers to your problems; and because your mind is calm, you are capable of picking out the best solution. Follow that solution, and you will meet with success. This is applying the science of religion in your daily life.

❖ ❖ ❖

"Human life is beset with sorrow until we know how to tune in with the Divine Will, whose 'right course' is often baffling to the egoistic intelligence," [Sri Yukteswar said]. "God alone gives unerring counsel; who but He bears the burden of the cosmos?"

❖ ❖ ❖

When we know the Heavenly Father, we will have the answers not only to our own problems, but to those that beset the world. Why do we live, and why do we die? Why the present happenings, and why those of the past? I doubt there will ever come on earth any saint who will answer all the questions of all human beings. But in the temple of meditation every riddle of life that troubles our hearts shall be resolved. We will learn the answers to the puzzles of life, and find the solution to all our difficulties, when we come in contact with God.

Affirmation

Heavenly Father, I will reason, I will will, I will act; but guide Thou my reason, will, and activity to the right thing that I should do.

CHAPTER 7

Achieving Your Goals

Nothing is impossible, unless you think it is.

❖ ❖ ❖

As a mortal being you are limited, but as a child of God you are unlimited....Focus your attention on God, and you shall have all the power you want, to use in any direction.

Using Dynamic Will Power

Will is the instrument of the image of God within you. In will lies His limitless power, the power that controls all the forces of nature. As you are made in His image, that power is yours to bring about whatever you desire.

❖ ❖ ❖

When you make up your mind to do good things, you will accomplish them if you use dynamic will power to follow through. No matter what the circumstances are, if you go on trying, God will create the means by which your will shall find its proper reward. This is the truth Jesus referred to when he said: "If ye have faith, and doubt not,...if ye shall say unto this mountain, Be thou removed, and be thou cast into the sea, it shall be done."* If you

* Matthew 21:21.

continuously use your will power, no matter what reverses come, it will produce success and health and power to help people, and above all, it will produce communion with God.

❖ ❖ ❖

Once you have said, "I will," never give in. If you say, "I will never catch cold," and the next morning you have a terrible cold and are discouraged, you are allowing your will to remain weak. You must not get discouraged when you see something happening that is contrary to what you have affirmed. Keep on believing, knowing it will be so. If outwardly you say, "I will," but inwardly think, "I can't," then you neutralize the power of thought and emasculate your will.

❖ ❖ ❖

If you want a home, and the mind says, "You simpleton, you can't afford a house," you must make your will stronger. When the "can't" disappears from your mind, divine power comes. A home will not be dropped down to you from heaven; you have to pour forth will power continuously through constructive actions. When you persist, refusing to accept failure, the object of will must materialize. When you continuously work that will through your thoughts and activities, what you are wishing for has to come about. Even though there is nothing in the world to conform to your wish, when your will persists, the desired result will somehow manifest.

❖ ❖ ❖

Mortal man's brain is full of "can'ts." Being born in a family with certain characteristics and habits, he is influenced by these to think he can't do certain things; he can't walk much, he can't eat this, he can't stand that. Those "can'ts" have to be cauterized. You have within you the power to accomplish everything you want; that power lies in the will.

❖ ❖ ❖

If you cling to a certain thought with dynamic will power, it finally assumes a tangible outward form.

❖ ❖ ❖

Carrying a thought with dynamic will power means holding to it until that thought pattern develops dynamic force. When a thought is made dynamic by will force, it can manifest according to the mental blueprint you have created.

❖ ❖ ❖

How can you develop will? Choose some objective that you think you cannot accomplish, and then try with all your might to do that one thing. When you have achieved success, go on to something bigger and keep on exercising your will power in this way. If your difficulty is great, deeply pray: "Lord, give me the power to conquer all my difficulties." You must use your will power, no matter what you are, or who you are. *You must make up your mind.* Use this will power both in business and in meditation.

❖ ❖ ❖

If, after calmly reasoning, you make up your mind that what you have set out to do is right, then nobody should be able to stop you. If I had no job I would shake up the whole world until people would say, "Give him a job to keep him quiet!"

❖ ❖ ❖

If you have convinced yourself that you are a helpless mortal, and you allow everyone else to convince you that you can't get a job, then you have passed the decree in your own mind that you are down and done for. No judgment from God or fate, but your own pronouncement on yourself, keeps you poor or worried. Success or failure is determined in your own mind. Even against the negative opinion of the rest of society, if you bring out by your all-conquering God-given will the conviction that you cannot be left to suffer in difficulties, you will feel a secret divine power coming upon you; and you will see that the magnetism of that conviction and power is opening up new ways for you.

Dealing Constructively With Failure

The season of failure is the best time for sowing the seeds of success. The bludgeon of circumstances may bruise you, but keep your head erect. Always try *once more,* no matter how many times you have failed. Fight when you think that you can fight no longer, or when you think that you have already done your best, or until your efforts are crowned with success.

❖ ❖ ❖

Learn how to use the psychology of victory. Some people advise, "Don't talk about failure at all." But that alone won't help. First, analyze your failure and its causes, benefit from the experience, and then dismiss all thought of it. Though he fail many times, the man who keeps on striving, who is undefeated within, is a truly victorious person.

❖ ❖ ❖

Life may be dark, difficulties may come, opportunities may slip by unutilized, but never within yourself say, "I am done for. God has forsaken me." Who could do anything for that kind of person? Your family may forsake you; good fortune may seemingly desert you; all the forces of man and nature may be arrayed against you; but by the quality of divine initiative within you, you can defeat every invasion of fate created by your own past wrong actions, and march victorious into paradise.

❖ ❖ ❖

If you are guided by the Divine Consciousness, then even when the future seems absolutely black, everything ultimately will come out all right. When God guides you, you cannot fail.

❖ ❖ ❖

You must banish the thought that the Lord with His wonderful power is far away in heaven, and that you are a helpless little worm buried in difficulties down here on earth. Remember that behind your will is the great Divine Will.

❖ ❖ ❖

To stumble and fall into wrong ways is only momentary weakness. Do not think yourself wholly lost. The same ground on which you fall can be used as a support to help you get up again, if you learn from your experiences.

❖ ❖ ❖

If you recognize a mistake and resolutely determine not to make it again, then even if you fall, that fall will be very much less than if you had never tried.

❖ ❖ ❖

When the winter of trials comes, some leaves of life fall away. This is normal. It doesn't matter. Take it in your stride. Say, "Never mind, summer is coming, and I shall blossom forth again." God has given inner strength for the tree to survive the harshest winters. You are no less endowed. The wintertimes of life come not to destroy you, but to stimulate you to fresh enthusiasm and constructive effort, which will blossom forth in the spring of new opportunities that come to everyone. You must say to yourself, "This wintertime of my life shall not last. I will get out of the grip of these trials, and I shall throw out new leaves and blossoms of improvements. And once more the bird of paradise shall sit on the branches of my life."

❖ ❖ ❖

No matter how many times you fail, keep on trying. No matter what happens, if you have unalterably resolved, "The earth may be shattered, but I will keep on doing the best I can," you are using dynamic will, and you will succeed. That dynamic will is what makes one man rich and another man strong and another man a saint.

Concentration: A Key to Success

The root cause of many failures in life is lack of concentration. Attention is like a searchlight; when its beam is spread over a vast area, its power to focus on a particular object becomes weak, but focused on one thing at a time, it becomes powerful. Great men are men of concentration. They put their whole mind on one thing at a time.

❖ ❖ ❖

One should know the scientific method of concentration* by which he may disengage his attention from objects of distraction and focus it upon one thing at a time. By the power of concentration, man can use the untold power of mind to accomplish that which he desires, and he can guard all doors through which failure may enter.

❖ ❖ ❖

* Taught in the *Self-Realization Fellowship Lessons*.

Many persons think that their actions have to be either restless or slow. That is not true. If you keep calm, with intense concentration, you will perform all duties with the correct speed.

❖ ❖ ❖

A calm person has his senses fully identified with the environment in which he places himself. A restless person does not notice anything; consequently he gets into trouble with himself and others and misunderstands everything....Never change the center of your concentration from calmness to restlessness. Perform activities only with concentration.

❖ ❖ ❖

Always center your whole mind on whatever you may be doing, however small or seemingly unimportant it may be. Also learn to keep your mind flexible so that you can transfer your attention at a moment's notice. But above all do everything with one hundred percent concentration.

❖ ❖ ❖

Most people do everything half-heartedly. They use only about one-tenth of their attention. That is why they haven't the power to succeed....[Do] everything with the power of attention. The full force of that power can be attained through meditation. When you use that focusing power of God, you can place it on anything and be a success.

Creativity

Tune yourself with the creative power of Spirit. You will be in contact with the Infinite Intelligence that is able to guide you and to solve all problems. Power from the dynamic Source of your being will flow uninterruptedly so that you will be able to perform creatively in any sphere of activity.

❖ ❖ ❖

Ask yourself this question: "Have I ever tried to do anything that nobody else has done?" That is the starting point in the application of initiative. If you haven't thought that far, you are like hundreds of others who erroneously think they have no power to act differently than they do. They are like sleepwalkers; the suggestions coming from their subconscious mind have given them the consciousness of one-horsepower people.

If you have been going through life in this somnambulistic state, you must wake yourself by affirming: "I have man's greatest quality—initiative. Every human being has some spark of power by which he can create something that has not been created before. Yet I see how easily I could be deluded with the mortal consciousness of limitation that pervades the world, if I allowed myself to be hypnotized by environment!"

❖ ❖ ❖

What is initiative? It is a creative faculty within you, a spark of the Infinite Creator. It may give you the power to create something no one else has ever created. It urges you to do things in new ways. The accomplishments of a person of initiative may be as spectacular as a shooting star. Apparently creating something from nothing, he demonstrates that the seemingly impossible may become possible by one's employment of the great inventive power of the Spirit.

❖ ❖ ❖

The one who creates does not wait for an opportunity, blaming circumstances, the fates, and the gods. He seizes opportunities or creates them with the magic wand of his will, effort, and searching discrimination.

❖ ❖ ❖

Before embarking on important undertakings, sit quietly, calm your senses and thoughts, and meditate deeply. You will then be guided by the great creative power of Spirit.

❖ ❖ ❖

Whatever you want to do, think about it until you are lost in that idea. Think, think, think, and make plans. Then take a little time; don't jump into anything at once. Take a step, and then think more. Something within tells you what to do. Do it, and think some more. Some further guidance will come. By learning to go deep within, you will connect your consciousness with the superconsciousness of the soul, so that with infinite will power, patience, and intuition you can grow those idea-seeds of success.

❖ ❖ ❖

As soon as you think a right thought, work it. Some people have a good idea but they haven't the tenacity to think it through and work it out. You must have courage and perseverance, and think, "I am going to see my idea through. It may be that I won't win out in this life, but I will make the effort." Think and act, think and act. That is how to develop your mind power. Every idea is a little seed, but you have to grow it.

❖ ❖ ❖

Many people try to achieve something in the realm of thought, but they give up when difficulties arise. Only those persons who have visualized their thoughts very strongly have been able to manifest them in outward form.

❖ ❖ ❖

Imagination [the power to image or visualize] is a very important factor in creative thought. But imagination has to be ripened into conviction. You can't do that without a strong will. But if you imagine something with all the power of your will, your imagination will be converted into conviction. And when you can hold that conviction against all odds, it will come true.

❖ ❖ ❖

Make mental blueprints of little things, and keep on making them materialize until you can make your big dreams also come true.

❖ ❖ ❖

Men of success are those who have forethought enough to make an indelible blueprint in their minds of whatever they wish to build or produce upon this earth. Backed by the financier of their creative ability, they employ their will power as contractor, their detailed attention as carpenters, and their mental patience as the necessary labor to materialize in true life the desired result or object.

❖ ❖ ❖

Whenever you want to produce something, do not depend upon the outside source; go deep and seek the Infinite Source. All methods of business success, all inventions, all vibrations of music, and all inspirational thoughts and writings are recorded in the annals of God.

❖ ❖ ❖

Work on your progress with God. This is the most important of all creative thinking.

Creating All-Round Success

He is the wisest who seeks God. He is the most successful who has found God.

❖ ❖ ❖

Success is not a simple matter; it cannot be determined merely by the amount of money and material possessions you have. The meaning of success goes far deeper. It can only be measured by the extent to which your inner peace and mental control enable you to be happy under all circumstances. That is real success.

❖ ❖ ❖

Great teachers will never counsel you to be neglectful; they will teach you to be balanced. You have to work, no doubt, to feed and clothe the body. But if you allow one duty to contradict another, it is not a true duty. Thousands of businessmen are so busy gathering wealth, they forget that they are creating a lot of heart disease too! If duty to prosperity makes you forget duty to health, it is not duty. One should develop in a harmonious way. There is no use giving special attention to developing a wonderful body, if it houses a peanut brain. The mind also must be developed. And if you have excellent health and prosperity and intellect, but you are not happy, then you have still not made a success of your life. When you can truthfully say, "I am happy, and no one can take my happiness away from me," you are a king—you have found the image of God within you.

❖ ❖ ❖

Another qualification of success is that we not only bring harmonious and beneficial results to ourselves, but also share those benefits with others.

❖ ❖ ❖

Life should be chiefly service. Without that ideal, the intelligence that God has given you is not reaching out toward its goal. When in service you forget the little self, you will feel the big Self of Spirit. As the vital rays of the sun nurture all, so should you spread rays of hope in the hearts of the poor and forsaken, kindle courage in the hearts of the despondent, and light a new strength in the hearts of those who think that they are failures. When you realize that life is a joyous battle of duty and at the same time a passing dream, and when you become filled with the joy of making others happy by giving them kindness and peace, in God's eyes your life is a success.

The Value of Enthusiasm

Work of any kind, if done in the right spirit, gives you victory over yourself....The attitude with which you work is what counts. Mental laziness and working unwillingly spoil one. People often ask me, "How do you do so many things?" It is because I do everything with the greatest pleasure and spirit of service. Inwardly I am all the time with God. And though I sleep very little I always feel fresh, because I perform my duties with the right attitude: that it is a privilege to serve.

❖ ❖ ❖

Mental unwillingness to work is accompanied by listlessness and lack of energy. Enthusiasm and willingness go hand in hand with fresh supplies of energy. From these facts we can see the subtle relationship between will and energy. The greater the will, the more inexhaustible the energy.

❖ ❖ ❖

If your work in life is humble, do not apologize for it. Be proud because you are fulfilling the duty given you by the Father. He needs you in your particular place; all people cannot play the same role. So long as you work to please God, all cosmic forces will harmoniously assist you.

❖ ❖ ❖

In God's eyes nothing is large or small. Were it not for His perfect nicety in constructing the tiny atom, could the skies wear the proud structures of Vega, Arcturus? Distinctions of "important" and "unimportant" are surely unknown to the Lord, lest, for want of a pin, the cosmos collapse!

❖ ❖ ❖

Try to do little things in an extraordinary way.

❖ ❖ ❖

You should progress—try to be the very best in your profession. Express the limitless power of soul in anything you take up....You must constantly create and produce new successes and not become [an] automaton. All work is purifying if done with the right motive.

❖ ❖ ❖

Concentration means to gather in your attention, focusing it to one point....Use that concentrated attention to do something quickly that ordinarily would take a long time.

❖ ❖ ❖

By stick-to-itiveness, by cultivating creative originality and developing your talents through the unlimited power of God that comes from communion with Him daily in deep meditation; by honest business methods, loyalty to your employer, and thinking of his business as if it were your own; and by cultivating an intuitive attunement with your immediate superior or with the owner of the business and with your Cosmic Employer—God—you may unfailingly please your employer in the office and your Divine Employer.

❖ ❖ ❖

It is easy to be idle or filled with hopelessness and thus desist from striving for financial success in life. It is easy to earn money dishonestly when such opportunity presents itself. But it is wrong thus to excuse oneself from making an effort to sustain himself honorably....

It is an exceptional man who earns money abundantly, unselfishly, honestly, quickly, just for God and His work and for making others happy. Such activity develops many sterling qualities of character that aid one on the spiritual path as well as the material path. Making money honestly and industriously to serve God's work is the next greatest art after the art of realizing God. Responsibility, knowledge of organization, order, leadership, and practical usefulness are developed in creating business success and are necessary for the all-round growth of man.

Abundance and Prosperity

Those who seek prosperity for themselves alone are in the end bound to become poor, or to suffer from mental inharmony; but those who consider the whole world as their home, and who really care and work for group or world prosperity...find the individual prosperity that is legitimately theirs. This is a sure and secret law.

❖ ❖ ❖

Unselfishness is the governing principle in the law of prosperity.

❖ ❖ ❖

I own nothing, yet I know that if I were hungry there would be thousands in the world who would feed me, because I have given to thousands. That same law will work for whoever thinks not of himself as the one who is going to starve, but of the other person in need.

❖ ❖ ❖

Every day, do some good to help others, even if it is only a pittance. If you want to love God you must love people. They are His children. You can be helpful materially by giving to the needy; and mentally by giving comfort to the sorrowful, courage to the fearful, divine friendship and moral support to the weak. You also sow seeds of goodness when you interest others in God, and cultivate in them greater love for God, deeper faith in Him. When you leave this world, material riches will be left behind;

but every good that you have done will go with you.
Wealthy people who live in miserliness, and selfish
people who never help others, do not attract wealth
in their next life. But those who give and share,
whether they have much or little, will attract prosperity. That is the law of God.

❖ ❖ ❖

Think of Divine Abundance as a mighty, refresh-
ing rain; whatever receptacle you have at hand will
receive it. If you hold up a tin cup, you will receive
only that quantity. If you hold up a bowl, that will
be filled. What kind of receptacle are you holding
up to Divine Abundance? Perhaps your vessel is de-
fective; if so, it should be repaired by casting out all
fear, hate, doubt, and envy, and then cleansed by the
purifying waters of peace, tranquility, devotion, and
love. Divine Abundance follows the law of service
and generosity. Give and then receive. Give to the
world the best you have and the best will come back
to you.

❖ ❖ ❖

Thanksgiving and praise open in your consciousness the way for spiritual growth and supply to come
to you. Spirit pushes Itself out into visible manifestation as soon as a channel is opened through which
It can flow.

❖ ❖ ❖

"To men who meditate on Me as their Very Own,
ever united to Me by incessant worship, I supply

their deficiencies and make permanent their gains."* [Those] who are faithful to their Creator, perceiving Him in all the diverse phases of life, discover that He has taken charge of their lives even in the smallest detail, and with divine foresight makes smooth their paths....

This stanza of the Gita reminds us of Christ's words: "But seek ye first the kingdom of God, and His righteousness; and all these things shall be added unto you."†

Affirmations for Success

I will go forth in perfect faith in the power of Omnipresent Good to bring me what I need at the time I need it.

❖ ❖ ❖

There is hidden strength within me to overcome all obstacles and temptations. I will bring forth that indomitable power and energy.

❖ ❖ ❖

I will thank God that I am able to try again and again, until with His help I do succeed. I will thank Him when I have succeeded in fulfilling my heart's worthy desire.

---

* Bhagavad Gita IX:22.
† Matthew 6:33.

Affirmations for Divine Abundance

O Father, I want prosperity, health, and wisdom without measure, not from earthly sources but from Thine all-possessing, all-powerful, all-bountiful hands.

I will not be a beggar, asking limited mortal prosperity, health, and knowledge. I am Thy child, and as such I demand, without limitations, a divine son's share of Thine illimitable riches.

❖ ❖ ❖

Divine Father, this is my prayer: I care not what I permanently possess, but give me power to acquire at will whatever I daily need.

CHAPTER 8

Inner Peace: Antidote for Stress, Worry, and Fear

Calmness is the ideal state in which we should receive all life's experiences. Nervousness is the opposite of calmness, and its prevalence today makes it very nearly a world disease.

❖ ❖ ❖

Those whose thoughts are inharmonious will always find inharmony. It is largely a perception from within, more than conditions without. Culture harmony within you, and you will spread it to others.... Everywhere you go, into the most incongruous circumstances, you will be able to find and nurture an underlying harmony.

❖ ❖ ❖

When you worry, there is static coming through your mind radio. God's song is the song of calmness. Nervousness is the static; calmness is the voice of God speaking to you through the radio of your soul.

❖ ❖ ❖

Calmness is the living breath of God's immortality in you.

❖ ❖ ❖

Everything you do should be done with peace.

That is the best medicine for your body, mind, and soul. It is the most wonderful way to live.

❖ ❖ ❖

Peace is the altar of God, the condition in which happiness exists.

❖ ❖ ❖

If you keep your mind on the resolve never to lose your peace, then you can attain godliness. Keep a secret chamber of silence within yourself, where you will not let moods, trials, battles, or inharmony enter. Keep out all hatred, revengefulness, and desires. In this chamber of peace God will visit you.

❖ ❖ ❖

You cannot buy peace; you must know how to manufacture it within, in the stillness of your daily practices in meditation.

❖ ❖ ❖

We should pattern our life by a triangular guide: calmness and sweetness are the two sides; the base is happiness. Every day, one should remind himself: "I am a prince of peace, sitting on the throne of poise, directing my kingdom of activity." Whether one acts quickly or slowly, in solitude or in the busy marts of men, his center should be peaceful, poised.

Nervousness

One who is naturally calm does not lose his

sense of reason, justice, or humor under any circumstances....He does not poison his bodily tissues with anger or fear, which adversely affect circulation. It is a well-proven fact that the milk of an angry mother can have a harmful effect on her child. What more striking proof can we ask for, that violent emotions will finally reduce the body to an ignominious wreck?

❖ ❖ ❖

Indulgence in constant thoughts of fear, anger, melancholy, remorse, envy, sorrow, hatred, discontent, or worry; and lack of the necessities for normal and happy living, such as right food, proper exercise, fresh air, sunshine, agreeable work and a purpose in life, all are causes of nervous disease.

❖ ❖ ❖

If we connect a 120-volt bulb with a 2,000-volt source, it would burn out the bulb. Similarly, the nervous system was not made to withstand the destructive force of intense emotion or persistent negative thoughts and feelings.

❖ ❖ ❖

But nervousness can be cured. The sufferer must be willing to analyze his condition and remove the disintegrating emotions and negative thoughts that are little by little destroying him. Objective analysis of one's problems,* and maintaining calmness in all

---

* See chapter 6.

situations of life will heal the most persistent case of nervousness....The victim of nervousness must understand his case, and must reflect on those continual mistakes of thinking which are responsible for his maladjustment to life.

❖ ❖ ❖

Instead of hurrying in a state of emotional excitement to get some place, and then not enjoying it once you arrive because you are restless, try to be more calm....As soon as your mind becomes restless, give it a whack with your will and order it to be calm.

❖ ❖ ❖

Excitement upsets the nervous balance, sending too much energy to some parts and depriving others of their normal share. This lack of proper distribution of nerve force is the sole cause of nervousness.

❖ ❖ ❖

A body that is relaxed and calm invites mental peace.

❖ ❖ ❖

[Technique* for relaxing the body:]

Tense with will: By command of will, direct the life energy (through the process of tension) to flood

* Simplified reference to a special technique developed in 1916 by Paramahansa Yogananda to recharge the body with vitality and to promote perfect relaxation; taught in *Self-Realization Fellowship Lessons.* The general principle of tensing and relaxing has in recent

the body or any body part. Feel the energy vibrating there, energizing and revitalizing. *Relax and feel:* Relax the tension, and feel the soothing tingle of new life and vitality in the recharged area. *Feel* that you are not the body; you are that life which sustains the body. *Feel* the peace, the freedom, the increased awareness that comes with the calmness produced by the practice of this technique.

❖ ❖ ❖

When you have peace in every movement of your body, and peace in your thinking, and in your will power, and peace in your love, and peace and God in your ambitions, remember—you have connected God with your life.

Worry and Fear

Although life seems capricious, uncertain, and full of all kinds of troubles, still we are always under the guiding, loving protection of God.

❖ ❖ ❖

Don't make a fuss about anything. Whenever you worry, remember, you are deepening the cosmic delusion within you.*

---

years been popularly endorsed and used by medical science as an aid in many maladies, including reduction of nervousness and high blood pressure.

* Man's forgetfulness of his true omnipotent soul nature, and of its divine connection with God, is the cause of all his suffering and

❖ ❖ ❖

Fear of failure or sickness is cultivated by turning over such thoughts in the conscious mind until they become rooted in the subconscious and finally in the superconscious.* Then the superconsciously and subconsciously rooted fear begins to germinate and fill the conscious mind with fear plants that are not so easy to destroy as the original thought would have been, and these eventually bear their poisonous, death-dealing fruits....

Uproot them from within by forceful concentration upon courage, and by shifting your consciousness to the absolute peace of God within.

❖ ❖ ❖

Whatever it is that you fear, take your mind away from it and leave it to God. Have faith in Him. Much suffering is due simply to worry. Why suffer now when the malady has not yet come? Since most of our ills come through fear, if you give up fear you will be free at once. The healing will be instant. Every night, before you sleep, affirm: "The Heavenly Father is with me; I am protected." Mentally surround yourself with Spirit....You will feel His wonderful protection.

❖ ❖ ❖

---

limitation. Yoga teaches that this oblivion or ignorance is caused by *maya,* or cosmic delusion.

* The higher mind from which the subconscious and conscious minds derive their power.

When the consciousness is kept on
have no fears; every obstacle will then be ov...
by courage and faith.

❖ ❖ ❖

Fear comes from the heart. If ever you feel overcome by dread of some illness or accident, you should
inhale and exhale deeply, slowly, and rhythmically
several times, relaxing with each exhalation. This
helps the circulation to become normal. If your heart
is truly quiet you cannot feel fear at all.

❖ ❖ ❖

Mental relaxation consists in the ability to free
the attention at will from nagging worries over past
and present difficulties; from constant awareness of
duty; from dread of accidents and other haunting
fears; and from greed, passion, or other disturbing
or negative thoughts and attachments. Mastery in
mental relaxation comes with faithful practice. It is
attained when one is able to rid the mind at will of
all restless thoughts and fix the attention fully on
the peace and contentment within.

❖ ❖ ❖

Forget the past, for it is gone from your domain!
Forget the future, for it is beyond your reach! Control the present! Live supremely well now! It will
whitewash the dark past, and compel the future to
be bright! This is the way of the wise.

❖ ❖ ❖

When we have too much to do at one time, we become very discouraged. Instead of worrying about what should be done, just say: "This hour is mine. I will do the best I can." The clock cannot tick twenty-four hours away in one minute, and you cannot do in one hour what you can do in twenty-four hours. Live each present moment completely and the future will take care of itself. Fully enjoy the wonder and beauty of each instant. Practice the presence of peace. The more you do that, the more you will feel the presence of that power in your life.

❖ ❖ ❖

The pleasure of modern man is in getting more and more, and what happens to anyone else doesn't matter. But isn't it better to live simply—without so many luxuries and with fewer worries? There is no pleasure in driving yourself until you cannot enjoy what you have....The time will come when mankind will begin to get away from the consciousness of needing so many material things. More security and peace will be found in the simple life.

❖ ❖ ❖

The inveterate worker who goes at it nonstop seven days a week lets his soul become subject to mechanical activity. Such a person loses his ability to govern his activity by free will, discrimination, and peace. He becomes a physical and mental wreck, shorn of spiritual happiness. Activity and calmness both must be cultivated and kept in balance, one with the other, in order to produce peace and happiness during periods of activity as well as silence.

❖ ❖ ❖

Observance of the Sabbath* as a day given to God and spiritual culture signifies the willing cessation of all activities that scatter and divert the mind into material channels....Spend the day in God-reminding, spiritually rejuvenating activities. With so many material enticements kept alive on Sabbath days, the minds of people run riot. Where is the time for restorative calmness, introspection, and creative thinking to adopt the best actions for an all-round existence during the coming week? A Sabbath well spent in silence, meditation, and creative thinking (not frantic reasonings but a stilling of thoughts, which are then replaced with intuitive perception) affords the soul reinforcement with harmony, peace, and mental and physical strength to use discrimination to develop physically, mentally, and spiritually in the best possible way.

❖ ❖ ❖

If you continually write out checks without depositing anything in your bank account, you will run out of money. So it is with your life. Without regular deposits of peace in your life account, you

* The word derives from Hebrew *shabath*, "to cease to do; to rest." A "Sabbath day" for spiritual regeneration need not be a particular day of the week; it may be beneficially observed on any day suited to one's circumstances or community tradition.

will run out of strength, calmness, and happiness. You will finally become bankrupt — emotionally, mentally, physically, and spiritually. But daily communion with God will continually replenish your inner bankroll.

❖ ❖ ❖

No matter how busy we are, we should not forget now and then to free our minds completely from worries and all duties....Try to remain for one minute at a time without thinking negatively, fixing the mind on the peace within, especially if worried. Then try to remain for several minutes with a quiet mind. Following that, think of some happy incident; dwell on it and visualize it; mentally go through some pleasant experience over and over again until you have forgotten your worries entirely.

❖ ❖ ❖

When beset by overwhelming mental trials or worries one should try to fall asleep. If he can do that, he will find upon awakening that the mental tension has been relieved, and that the worry has loosened its grip.* We need to remind ourselves at such times that even if we died, the earth would continue to follow its orbit, and business would be carried on as usual; so why worry?

---

* As explained on page 18, by going into the subconscious state of sleep the soul temporarily rises above troubles associated with attachment to the body and its experiences. An even greater method is to enter the superconscious state of communion with God through deep meditation.

❖ ❖ ❖

Life is entertaining when we do not take it too seriously. A good laugh is an excellent remedy for human ills. One of the best characteristics of the American people is their ability to laugh. To be able to laugh at life is marvelous. This my master [Swami Sri Yukteswar] taught me. In the beginning of my training in his hermitage, I went about with a solemn face, never smiling. One day Master pointedly remarked, "What is this? Are you attending a funeral ceremony? Don't you know that finding God is the funeral of all sorrows? Then why so glum? Don't take this life too seriously."

❖ ❖ ❖

Knowing that you are a child of God, make up your mind to be calm no matter what happens. If your mind is fully identified with your activities, you cannot be conscious of the Lord, but if you are calm and receptive to Him within while being active without, you are rightly active.

❖ ❖ ❖

Through meditation one can experience a stable, silent inner peace that can be a permanently soothing background for all harmonious or trialsome activities demanded by life's responsibilities. Lasting happiness lies in maintaining this evenly peaceful state of mind, even when worries seek to unsettle the inner equanimity, or success tries to excite the mind to abnormal elation.

A lump of sand cannot withstand the erosive effect of the ocean's waves; an individual who lacks
imperturbable inner peace cannot remain tranquil
during mental conflict. But as a diamond remains
unchanged no matter how many waves swirl around
it, so also a peace-crystallized individual remains ra-
diantly serene even when trials beset him from all
sides. Out of the changeful waters of life, let us sal-
vage through meditation the diamond of unchangeable soul-consciousness, which sparkles with the
everlasting joy of Spirit.*

❖ ❖ ❖

Realization that all power to think, speak, feel,
and act comes from God, and that He is ever with us,
inspiring and guiding us, brings an instant freedom
from nervousness. Flashes of divine joy will come
with this realization; sometimes a deep illumination will pervade one's being, banishing the very concept of fear. Like an ocean, the power of God sweeps
in, surging through the heart in a cleansing flood,

---

* "The state of complete tranquility of the feeling (*chitta*), attained
by yoga meditation, in which the self (ego) perceives itself as the Self
(soul) and is content (fixed) in the Self;

"The state in which the sense-transcendent immeasurable bliss
becomes known to the awakened intuitive intelligence, and in which
the yogi remains enthroned, never again to be removed;

"The state that, once found, the yogi considers as the treasure
beyond all other treasures—anchored therein, he is immune to even
the mightiest grief;

"That state is known as yoga—the pain-free state. The practice of
yoga is therefore to be observed resolutely and with a stout heart."
(Bhagavad Gita VI:20–23).

removing all obstructions of delusive doubt, nervousness, and fear. The delusion of matter, the consciousness of being only a mortal body, is overcome by contacting the sweet serenity of Spirit, attainable by daily meditation. Then you know that the body is a little bubble of energy in His cosmic sea.

Affirmations for Peace and Calmness

I am a prince of peace, sitting on the throne of poise, directing the kingdom of activity.

❖ ❖ ❖

The moment I am restless or disturbed in mind, I will retire to silence and meditation until calmness is restored.

❖ ❖ ❖

I will be neither lazy nor feverishly active. In every challenge of life I shall do my best without worrying about the future.

CHAPTER 9

Bringing Out the Best Within You

We are what we *think* we are. The habitual inclination of our thoughts determines our talents and abilities, and our personality. Thus, some *think* they are writers or artists, industrious or lazy, and so on. What if you want to be other than what you presently think you are? You may argue that others have been born with the special talent you lack but desire to have. This is true. But they had to cultivate the habit of that ability some time—if not in this life, then in a previous one.* So whatever you want to be, start to develop that pattern now. You can instill any trend in your consciousness right now, provided you inject a strong thought in your mind; then your actions and whole being will obey that thought.

❖ ❖ ❖

One must never give up hope of becoming better. A person is old only when he refuses to make the effort to change. That stagnant state is the only "old age" I recognize. When a person says again and again, "I can't change; this is the way I am," then I have to say, "All right, stay that way, since you have made up your mind to be like that."

* See *reincarnation* in glossary.

❖ ❖ ❖

No matter what his present state, man can change for the better through self-control, discipline, and following proper diet and health laws. Why do you think you cannot change? Mental laziness is the secret cause of all weakness.

❖ ❖ ❖

Everyone has self-limiting idiosyncrasies. These were not put into your nature by God, but were created by you. These are what you must change—by remembering that these habits, peculiar to your nature, are nothing but manifestations of your own thoughts.

❖ ❖ ❖

In the ultimate sense, all things are made of pure consciousness; their finite appearance is the result of the relativity of consciousness.* Therefore, if you want to change anything in yourself, you must change the process of thought that occasions the materialization of consciousness into different forms of

---

* Yoga teaches that the thought of God is the fundamental structure of creation. Just as steam becomes water by condensation, and by further condensation becomes ice, all patterns and forms of energy and matter are condensations of consciousness. Pioneering physicists of the twentieth century are rediscovering what the yogis have known since ancient times. Sir James Jeans, British scientist, wrote: "The universe begins to look more like a great thought than like a great machine." And Einstein said: "I want to know how God created this world. I am not interested in this or that phenomenon, in the spectrum of this or that element. I want to know His thoughts; the rest are details."

matter and action. That is the way, the only way, to remold your life.

❖ ❖ ❖

Look within and determine your main characteristics....Don't try to change in yourself what is good. But those things you do against your will, and that make you unhappy after you have done them, are what you want to get rid of. How? Affirm with conviction, before going to bed and on arising in the morning, "I can change. I have the will to change. I *will* change!" Hold to that thought throughout the day, and carry it with you into the subconscious land of sleep and the superconscious realm of meditation.

❖ ❖ ❖

Very simply, all you have to do is to think away the thoughts you want to destroy, by replacing them with constructive thoughts. This is the key to heaven; it is in your hands.

Introspection: A Secret of Progress

The first thing to do is to introspect. Take stock of yourself and your habits, and find out what is standing in your way. Often it is inertia, or lack of definite, undivided effort and attention. Sometimes there are habits that need to be weeded out of the garden of your life, so that true happiness may become more firmly rooted.

❖ ❖ ❖

One secret of progress is self-analysis. Introspection is a mirror in which to see recesses of your mind that otherwise would remain hidden from you. Diagnose your failures and sort out your good and bad tendencies. Analyze what you are, what you wish to become, and what shortcomings are impeding you.

❖ ❖ ❖

Millions of people never analyze themselves. Mentally they are mechanical products of the factory of their environment, preoccupied with breakfast, lunch, and dinner, working and sleeping, and going here and there to be entertained. They don't know what or why they are seeking, nor why they never realize complete happiness and lasting satisfaction. By evading self-analysis, people go on being robots, conditioned by their environment. True self-analysis is the greatest art of progress.

Everyone should learn to analyze himself dispassionately. Write down your thoughts and aspirations daily. Find out what you are—not what you imagine you are!—because you want to make yourself what you ought to be. Most people don't change because they don't see their own faults.

❖ ❖ ❖

One who has not kept a mental diary should begin this salutary practice. The knowledge of just how much and in what way he fails in the daily experiences of life may stimulate him to more effort to be what he should be. By keeping such a journal and by using discrimination to destroy the bad habits that create pain and suffering for ourselves and others, we will get rid of them. Every night we should ask ourselves: "How long have I been with God today?" We should analyze also how much we have deeply thought, how much we have accomplished in our duties, how much we have done for others, how we have governed ourselves in the various situations of the day.

❖ ❖ ❖

By watching the graphs of your mind, you can see whether you are progressing every day. You don't want to hide from yourself. You must know yourself as you are. By keeping a diary of your introspection, you keep watch on your bad habits and are better prepared to destroy them.

Conquering Temptations

Sometimes it seems difficult to be good, while it is easy to be bad; and that to give up the bad things is to miss something. But I say you will not miss anything but sorrow.

❖ ❖ ❖

Everything that the great ones have warned against is like poisoned honey. I say don't taste it. You may argue, "But it is sweet." Well, my reasoning is that after you have tasted the sweetness it will destroy you. Evil was made sweet to delude you. You have to use your discrimination to distinguish between poisoned honey and that which is in your best interest. Avoid those things that will ultimately hurt you, and choose those that will give you freedom and happiness.

❖ ❖ ❖

Sorrow, illness, and failure are natural results of transgressions against God's laws. Wisdom consists in avoiding such violations and finding peace and happiness within yourself through thoughts and actions that are in harmony with your real Self.

❖ ❖ ❖

Whenever there is an overwhelming desire in your heart...use your discrimination. Ask yourself, "Is it a good desire or a bad desire for which I seek fulfillment?"

❖ ❖ ❖

Material desires encourage our bad habits by engendering false hopes of satisfaction and happiness. At such times one should summon his discriminative powers to reveal the truth: Bad habits lead ultimately to unhappiness. Thus exposed, bad habits become impotent to hold man in their misery-making sway.

❖ ❖ ❖

Resisting temptations isn't the denial of all the pleasures of life; it is to have supernal control over what you want to do. I am showing you the way to real freedom, not the false sense of freedom that in

fact is compelling you to do what your habits lead
you to do.

❖ ❖ ❖

The old orthodox way is to deny temptation, to
suppress it. But you must learn to *control* that temptation. It is not a sin to be tempted. Even though you
are boiling with temptation, you are not evil; but if
you yield to that temptation, you are caught temporarily by the power of evil. You must erect about
yourself protecting parapets of wisdom. There is no
stronger force that you can employ against temptation than wisdom. Complete understanding will
bring you to the point where nothing can tempt you
to actions that promise pleasure but in the end will
only hurt you.

❖ ❖ ❖

Until you have attained wisdom, when temptation comes you must first stop the action or urge,
and *then* reason. If you try to reason first, you will
be compelled in spite of yourself to do the thing that
you don't want to do, because temptation will overcome all reason. Just say "No!" and get up and go
away. That is the surest way to escape the Devil.*
The more you develop this "won't" power during
the intrusion of temptation, the happier you will be;
for all joy depends on the ability to do that which
conscience tells you you *should* do.

---

* Satan; the conscious force of delusion that attempts to keep man
in ignorance of his divine nature. See *maya* in glossary.

❖ ❖ ❖

When you say *no* to temptation, you must mean *no*. Don't give in. The spineless weakling all the time says *yes*. But great minds are full of *no*s.

❖ ❖ ❖

When you have made up your mind not to smoke, or eat unwisely, or lie or cheat, be firm in these good desires; don't weaken. Wrong environment saps your will and invites wrong desires. Live with thieves and you think that is the only life. But live with divine persons, and after having divine communion, no other desires can tempt you.

❖ ❖ ❖

If you have a particular bad habit or karmic inclination, don't mix with those who have the same kind of bad habit. If you tend to be greedy, avoid the company of others who are greedy. If you have a desire to drink, stay away from those who drink. People who support your bad habits are not your friends. They will cause you to throw away your soul's joy. Avoid the company of wrongdoers and mix with those who are good.

❖ ❖ ❖

The greatest influence in your life, stronger even than your will power, is your environment. Change that, if necessary.

❖ ❖ ❖

There are two kinds of environment that you should watch carefully—the outer and the inner.

❖ ❖ ❖

Watch your thoughts. All your experiences come percolating through your thoughts. It is the company of your thoughts that uplifts or degrades you.

❖ ❖ ❖

You must be stronger than the thoughts and suggestions constantly vibrating from other people. That is the way to conquer wrong vibrations that come into your environment.

❖ ❖ ❖

Think of God as your environment. Be one with God and nothing can harm you.

❖ ❖ ❖

Every action has a mental counterpart. We perform acts with our physical power, but that activity has its origin in the mind, and is guided by the mental captain. To steal is evil; but the greater evil is the mental act of stealing that initiates the physical theft, because mind is the real perpetrator. Whatever wrong action you want to avoid, first throw it out of the mind. If you concentrate only on the physical action, it is very hard to gain control. Concentrate on the mind: correct your thoughts, and automatically the actions will be taken care of.

❖ ❖ ❖

Every time a bad thought comes, cast it out. Then Satan can't do anything to you. But as soon as you think wrongly, you go toward Satan. You are constantly moving back and forth between good and evil; to escape, you must go where Satan will be unable to reach you: deep in the heart of God.

❖ ❖ ❖

Virtue and purity are not rooted in weakness. Rather, they are strong qualities that fight the forces of evil. It is within your power to choose how much purity, love, beauty, and spiritual joy you will express, not only through deeds, but in your thoughts, feelings, and desires....Keep a pure mind and you will find the Lord ever with you. You will hear Him talking to you in the language of your heart; you will glimpse Him in every flower and shrub, in every blade of grass, in every passing thought. "Blessed are the pure in heart: for they shall see God."*

❖ ❖ ❖

The best way to overcome temptation is by comparison. Meditate more and see if meditation doesn't give you more happiness.

❖ ❖ ❖

When you withdraw your mind inward [in meditation], you will begin to perceive that there are many more wonderful things within than outside.

❖ ❖ ❖

If you but *looked* at your soul, the all-perfect

---

* Matthew 5:8.

reflection of God within you, you would find all your desires satisfied!

❖ ❖ ❖

In the absence of inward joy, men turn to evil. Meditation on the God of Bliss permeates us with goodness.

❖ ❖ ❖

The ego attempts to satisfy through material channels the soul's constant, insatiable longing for God. Far from accomplishing its objective, it increases man's misery. The soul's hunger can never be appeased by indulgence of the senses. When man realizes this and masters his ego, that is, when he achieves self-control, his life becomes glorified by the awareness of divine bliss while he is still in the flesh. Then, instead of being the slave of material desires and appetites, man's attention is transferred to the heart of Omnipresence, resting there forever with the hidden Joy in everything.

The Correct Attitude Toward Past Wrongs

Avoid dwelling on all the wrong things you have done. They do not belong to you now. Let them be forgotten. It is attention that creates habit and memory. As soon as you put the needle on a phonograph record, it begins to play. Attention is the needle that plays the record of past actions. So you should not put your attention on bad ones. Why go on suffering over the unwise actions of your past? Cast their memory from your mind, and take care not to repeat those actions again.

❖ ❖ ❖

You may be worried about the wrong you have committed, but God is not. What is past is past. You are His child, and whatever wrong you have done came about because you didn't know Him. He doesn't hold against you the evil done under the influence of ignorance. All He asks is that you not repeat your wrong actions. He wants only to find out whether or not you are sincere in your intention to be good.

❖ ❖ ❖

"Forget the past," [Sri Yukteswar said]. "The vanished lives of all men are dark with many shames. Human conduct is ever unreliable until man is anchored in the Divine. Everything in future will improve if you are making a spiritual effort now."

❖ ❖ ❖

Don't think of yourself as a sinner. You are a child of the Heavenly Father. No matter if you are the greatest sinner, forget it. If you have made up your mind to be good, then you are no longer a sinner....* Start with a clean slate and say: "I have

---

* "Even he with the worst of karma who ceaselessly meditates on Me quickly loses the effects of his past bad actions. Becoming a high-souled being, he soon attains perennial peace. Know this for certain: the devotee who puts his trust in Me never perishes!" (Bhagavad Gita IX:30–31).

always been good; I was only dreaming that I was bad." It is true: evil is a nightmare and does not belong to the soul.

❖ ❖ ❖

Though your errors be as deep as the ocean, the soul itself cannot be swallowed up by them. Have unflinching determination to move on your path unhampered by limiting thoughts of past errors.

❖ ❖ ❖

You are a spark of an Eternal Flame. You can hide the spark, but you can never destroy it.

❖ ❖ ❖

Darkness may reign in a cave for thousands of years, but bring in the light, and the darkness vanishes as though it had never been. Similarly, no matter what your defects, they are yours no longer when you bring in the light of goodness. So great is the light of the soul that incarnations of evil cannot destroy it.

❖ ❖ ❖

No sin is unforgivable, no evil insuperable; for the world of relativity does not contain absolutes.

❖ ❖ ❖

God never forsakes anyone. When, having sinned, you believe your guilt to be measureless, beyond redemption; and when the world declares you of no account and says you will never amount to anything, stop a moment to think of the Divine Mother.* Say to Her, "Divine Mother, I am Your child, Your naughty child. Please forgive me." When you appeal to the mother aspect of God there is no retort—you simply melt the Divine Heart. But God will not support you if you continue to do wrong. You must forsake your evil actions as you pray.

❖ ❖ ❖

Saints are sinners who did not give up. No matter what your difficulties, if you do not give up, you are making progress in your struggle against the stream. To struggle is to win the favor of God.

❖ ❖ ❖

Is a diamond less valuable because it is covered with mud? God sees the changeless beauty of our souls. He knows we are not our mistakes.

❖ ❖ ❖

For a few incarnations you have been a human being, but throughout eternity you have been a child of God. Never think of yourself as a sinner, because sin and ignorance are only mortal nightmares. When we will awaken in God, we will find that we—the soul, the pure consciousness—never did anything wrong. Untainted by mortal experiences, we are and ever have been the sons of God.

❖ ❖ ❖

* See glossary.

Each of us is a child of God. We are born of His spirit, in all its purity and glory and joy. That heritage is unassailable. To condemn oneself as a sinner, committed to the path of error, is the greatest of all sins. The Bible says: "Know ye not that ye are the temple of God, and that the Spirit of God dwelleth in you?"* Always remember: your Father loves you unconditionally.

Creating Good Habits and Destroying Bad Ones

Turn toward God and you will find yourself shaking off the chains of habits and environment.... The Self identified with the ego is bound; the Self identified with the soul is free.

❖ ❖ ❖

The mind may tell you that you cannot free yourself from a particular habit; but habits are nothing but repetitions of your own thoughts, and these you have the capacity to change.

❖ ❖ ❖

Most people who make up their minds to stop smoking or to stop eating so many sweets will

* I Corinthians 3:16. Cf. Bhagavad Gita XIII:22, 32: "The Supreme Spirit, transcendent and existing in the body, is the detached Beholder, the Consenter, the Sustainer, the Experiencer, the Great Lord, and also the Highest Self....The Self, though seated everywhere in the body, is ever taintless."

continue with those actions in spite of themselves. They do not change because their minds, like blotting paper, have soaked up habits of thought. Habit means that the mind believes it cannot get rid of a particular thought. Habit, indeed, is tenacious. Once you perform an action, it leaves an effect or impression on the consciousness. As a result of this influence, you are likely to repeat that action.

❖ ❖ ❖

Repeated performance of an action creates a mental blueprint. Every action is performed mentally as well as physically, and repetition of a particular action and its accompanying thought-pattern causes the formation of subtle electrical pathways in the physiological brain, somewhat like the grooves in a phonograph record. After a time, whenever you put the needle of attention on those "grooves" of electrical pathways, it plays back the "record" of the original mental blueprint. Each time an action is repeated, these grooves of electrical pathways become deeper, until the slightest attention automatically "plays" those same actions over and over again.

❖ ❖ ❖

These patterns make you behave in a certain way, often against your wish. Your life follows those grooves that you yourself have created in the brain. In that sense you are not a free person; you are more or less a victim of the habits you have formed. Depending on how set those patterns are, to that degree you are a puppet. But you can *neutralize* the dictates of those bad habits. How? By creating brain patterns of opposite good habits. And you can completely *erase* the grooves of bad habits by meditation.

❖ ❖ ❖

You must cure yourself of evil habits by cauterizing them with the opposite good habits. For instance, if you have a bad habit of telling lies and by doing so have lost many friends, start the opposite good habit of telling the truth.

❖ ❖ ❖

Weaken a bad habit by avoiding everything that occasioned it or stimulated it, without concentrating upon it in your zeal to avoid it. Then divert your mind to some good habit and steadily cultivate it until it becomes a dependable part of you.

❖ ❖ ❖

It takes time for even a bad habit to attain supremacy, so why be impatient about the growth of a rival good habit? Do not despair about your undesirable habits; simply stop feeding them and thus making them strong by repetition. The time that elapses in the formation of habits varies with individual nervous systems and brains and is chiefly determined by the quality of attention.

❖ ❖ ❖

Through the power of deep, concentration-trained attention, any habit may be installed—that is, new

patterns may be made in the brain—almost instan-
taneously and at will.

❖ ❖ ❖

When you want to create a good habit or destroy
a bad one, concentrate on the brain cells, the storehouse of the mechanisms of habits. To create a good
habit, meditate; and then with the concentration
fixed at the Christ center, the center of will between
the eyebrows, deeply affirm the good habit that you
want to install. And when you want to destroy bad
habits, concentrate at the Christ center and deeply
affirm that all the grooves of bad habits are being
erased.

❖ ❖ ❖

By concentration and will power you can erase
even deep grooves of long-standing habits. If you are
addicted to smoking, for example, say to yourself:
"The habit of smoking has long been lodged in my
brain. Now I put all my attention and concentration
on my brain and I *will* that habit to be dislodged."
Command your mind thus, again and again. The best
time of the day to do this is in the morning, when
the will and attention are fresh. Repeatedly affirm
your freedom, using all the strength of your will
power. One day you will suddenly feel that you no
longer are ensnared by that habit.

❖ ❖ ❖

If you really want to rid yourself of present bad habits...you have no greater recourse than meditation. Every time you meditate deeply on God, beneficial changes take place in the patterns of your brain.

❖ ❖ ❖

Meditate upon the thought, "I and my Father are one," trying to feel a great peace, and then a great joy in your heart. When that joy comes, say, "Father, Thou art with me. I command Thy power within me to cauterize my brain cells of wrong habits and past seed tendencies." The power of God in meditation will do it. Rid yourself of the limiting consciousness that you are a man or a woman; *know* that you are the child of God. Then mentally affirm and pray to God: "I command my brain cells to change, to destroy the grooves of bad habits that have made a puppet out of me. Lord, burn them up in Thy divine light."

❖ ❖ ❖

Suppose your problem is that you frequently get angry, and afterwards feel very sorry for having lost your temper. Every night and morning make up your mind to avoid anger, and then watch yourself carefully. The first day may be difficult, but the second may be a little easier. The third will be easier still. After a few days you will see that victory is possible. In a year, if you keep up your effort, you will be another person.

Prayer for Discriminative Wisdom

Give me the wisdom to follow happily the ways of righteousness. May I develop the soul faculty of discrimination that detects evil, in even its subtlest forms; and that guides me to the humble paths of goodness.

Affirmation for Removing Bad Habits

[Paramahansa Yogananda concluded one of his public talks on overcoming habits by addressing his listeners as follows:]

Close your eyes and think of one bad habit you want to get rid of....Affirm with me: "I am free of that habit now! I am free!" Hold on to that thought of freedom; forget the bad habit.

Repeat after me, "I shall remold my consciousness. In this new year I am a new person. And I shall change my consciousness again and again until I have driven away all the darkness of ignorance and manifested the shining light of Spirit in whose image I am made."

Prayer

O Divine Teacher, let me realize that though the gloom of my ignorance be age-old, with the dawn of Thy light the darkness will vanish as though it had never been.

CHAPTER 10

Happiness

If you have given up hope of ever being happy, cheer up. Never lose hope. Your soul, being a reflection of the ever joyous Spirit, is, in essence, happiness itself.

❖ ❖ ❖

If it is happiness you want, have it! There is nothing that can stop you.

Positive Mental Attitudes

Happiness depends to some extent upon external conditions, but chiefly upon mental attitudes.

❖ ❖ ❖

According to spiritual science, the attitude of the mind is everything....Train the mind to remain neutral to every condition. Mind is just like blotting paper, which readily takes on the color of any dye you apply to it. Most minds take on the color of their environment. But there is no excuse for the mind to be defeated by outer circumstances. If your mental attitude changes constantly under the pressure of tests, you are losing the battle of life.

❖ ❖ ❖

A strong determination to be happy will help you. Do not wait for your circumstances to change, thinking falsely that in them lies the trouble.

❖ ❖ ❖

Change your thoughts if you wish to change your circumstances. Since you alone are responsible for your thoughts, only you can change them. You will want to change them when you realize that each thought creates according to its own nature. Remember that the law works at all times and that you are always demonstrating according to the kind of thoughts you habitually entertain. Therefore, start now to think only those thoughts that will bring you health and happiness.

❖ ❖ ❖

Man needs to understand that his own intelligence controls the atoms of his body. He should not live in a closed chamber of mental narrowness. Breathe in the fresh air of vital thoughts and views of other people. Expel poisonous thoughts of discouragement, discontentment, hopelessness. Drink vitality and receive mental nourishment from materially and spiritually progressive minds. Feast unstintingly on the creative thinking within yourself and others. Take long mental walks on the path of self-confidence. Exercise with the instruments of judgment, introspection, and initiative.

❖ ❖ ❖

The mind, being the brain, feeling, and perception of all living cells, can keep the human body alert or depressed. The mind is the king, and all its cellular subjects behave exactly according to the mood of their royal master. Just as we concern ourselves with the nutritive value of our daily food menus, so should we consider the nutritive potency of the psychological menus that we daily serve the mind.

❖ ❖ ❖

The soul's nature is bliss: a lasting, inner state of ever-new, ever-changing joy....Establish your wayward consciousness in the changeless calm within you, which is the throne of God; then let your soul manifest bliss night and day.

❖ ❖ ❖

If you do not choose to be happy no one can make you happy. Do not blame God for that! And if you choose to be happy, no one can make you unhappy. If He had not given us freedom to use our own will, we could blame Him when we are unhappy, but He did give us that freedom. It is we who make of life what it is.

❖ ❖ ❖

Often we continue to suffer without making an effort to change; that is why we don't find lasting peace and contentment. If we would persevere we would certainly be able to conquer all difficulties. We must make the effort, that we may go from misery to happiness, from despondency to courage.

❖ ❖ ❖

The laughter of the infinite God must vibrate through your smile. Let the breeze of God's love spread your smiles in the hearts of men. Your divine smiles will be contagious; their fire will chase the gloom from others' hearts.

❖ ❖ ❖

Persons of strong character are usually the happiest. They do not blame others for troubles that can usually be traced to their own actions and lack of understanding. They know that no one has any power to add to their happiness or detract from it unless they themselves are so weak that they allow the adverse thoughts and wicked actions of others to affect them.

❖ ❖ ❖

Remember: no matter how wrong everything has gone for you, you have no right to be moody. In your *mind* you can be a conqueror. When bested, the moody man admits defeat. But the man whose mind remains unconquered, though the world be in cinders at his feet, is yet the victor.

❖ ❖ ❖

Your highest happiness lies in your being ever ready in desiring to learn, and to behave properly. The more you improve yourself, the more you will elevate others around you. The self-improving man is the increasingly happy man. The happier you become, the happier will be the people around you.

❖ ❖ ❖

Avoid a negative approach to life. Why gaze

down the sewers when there is loveliness all around us? One may find some fault in even the greatest masterpieces of art, music, and literature. But isn't it better to enjoy their charm and glory?

❖ ❖ ❖

Nearly everyone is familiar with those three little monkey-figures that depict the maxim, "See no evil, hear no evil, speak no evil." I emphasize the positive approach: "See that which is good, hear that which is good, speak that which is good."

❖ ❖ ❖

Good and evil, the positive and the negative, both exist in this world. While trying to keep the consciousness positive, many people become unreasonably afraid of negative thoughts. It is useless to deny that negative thoughts exist, but neither should you fear them. Use your discrimination to analyze wrong thoughts; and then dump them.

❖ ❖ ❖

Life has a bright side and a dark side, for the world of relativity is composed of light and shadows. If you permit your thoughts to dwell on evil, you yourself will become ugly. Look only for the good in everything, that you absorb the quality of beauty.

❖ ❖ ❖

Thinking, reading, and repeating statements of truth with deep attention will help to clear away negation and to establish a positive attitude in your mind. Repeat your prayers and affirmations with deep concentration until you establish a habit of thought, until it becomes as natural for you to think in the right way as it previously was for you to think negatively.

Freedom From Negative Moods

The ever new joy of God inherent in the soul is indestructible. So also, its expression in the mind can never be destroyed if one knows how to hold on to it, and if he does not deliberately change his mind and become sorrowful by nurturing moods.

❖ ❖ ❖

You are an image of God; you should behave like a god. But what happens? First thing in the morning you lose your temper and complain, "My coffee is cold!" What does it matter? Why be disturbed by such things? Have that evenness of mind wherein you are absolutely calm, free from all anger. That is what you want. Don't let anyone or anything "get your goat." Your "goat" is your peace. Let nothing take it away from you.

❖ ❖ ❖

Resurrect yourself from the littleness of life, the little things that disturb you.

❖ ❖ ❖

Nobody *likes* misery. Why not analyze yourself

next time you are in a mood? You will see how you are willingly, willfully making yourself miserable. And while you are doing so, others around you feel the unpleasantness of your state of mind....You must remove moods from your mental mirror.

❖ ❖ ❖

Always think of your mind as a garden, and keep it beautiful and fragrant with divine thoughts; let it not become a mud pond, rank with malodorous hateful moods. If you cultivate the heavenly scented blooms of peace and love, the bee of Christ Consciousness* will steal into your garden. As the bee seeks out only those flowers that are sweet with honey, so God comes only when your life is sweet with honeyed thoughts.

❖ ❖ ❖

Each type of mood has a specific cause, and it lies within your own mind.

❖ ❖ ❖

One should introspect each day in order to understand the nature of his mood, and how to correct it, if it is a harmful one. Perhaps you find yourself in an indifferent state of mind. No matter what is suggested, you are not interested. It is necessary then to make a conscious effort to create some positive

---

* God's consciousness, omnipresent in creation. See glossary.

interest. Beware of indifference, which ossifies your progress in life by paralyzing your will power.

Perhaps your mood is discouragement over sickness; a feeling that you will never regain health. You must try to apply the laws of right living that lead to a healthy, active, and moral life, and pray for greater faith in the healing power of God.

Or suppose your mood is a conviction that you are a failure, and can never succeed at anything. Analyze the problem and see if you have really made all the effort you could have.

❖ ❖ ❖

You can conquer your moods, no matter how terrible they seem. Make up your mind that you are not going to be moody anymore; and if a mood comes in spite of your resolve, analyze the cause that brought it on, and do something constructive about it.

❖ ❖ ❖

Creative thinking* is the best antidote for moods. Moods get their grip on your consciousness when you are in a negative or passive state of mind. The time when your mind is vacant is just the time it can become moody; and when you are moody, the devil comes and wields his influence on you. Therefore, develop creative thinking. Whenever you are

---

* See also pages 75–78.

not active physically, do something creative in your mind. Keep it so busy that you have no time to indulge in moodiness.

❖ ❖ ❖

When you are thinking creatively, you don't feel the body or moods; you become attuned with Spirit. Our human intelligence is made in the image of His creative intelligence, through which all things are possible; and if we don't live in that consciousness, we become a bundle of moods. By thinking creatively we destroy those moods.

❖ ❖ ❖

Remember that when you are unhappy it is generally because you do not visualize strongly enough the great things that you definitely want to accomplish in life, nor do you employ steadfastly enough your will power, your creative ability, and your patience until your dreams are materialized.

❖ ❖ ❖

Keep busy doing constructive things for your own self-improvement and for the benefit of others, for whoever would enter God's kingdom must try also to do good for others every day. If you follow this pattern, you will feel the mood-dispelling joy of knowing you are advancing, mentally, physically, and spiritually.

Service to Others

Happiness lies in making others happy, in forsaking self-interest to bring joy to others.

❖ ❖ ❖

Giving happiness to others is tremendously important to our own happiness, and a most satisfying experience. Some people think only of their own family: "Us four and no more." Others think only of self: "How am *I* going to be happy?" But these are the very persons who do not become happy!

❖ ❖ ❖

To live for self is the source of all misery.

❖ ❖ ❖

In being of spiritual, mental, and material service to others, you will find your own needs fulfilled. As you forget *self* in service to others, you will find that, without seeking it, your own cup of happiness will be full.

❖ ❖ ❖

When you came into this world, you cried and everyone else smiled. You should so live your life that when you leave, everyone else will cry, but you will be smiling.

❖ ❖ ❖

The deeper you meditate and the more willingly you serve, the happier you will be.

The Inner Conditions of Happiness

Learn to carry all the conditions of happiness within yourself by meditating and attuning your consciousness to the ever-existing, ever-conscious, ever-new Joy, which is God. Your happiness should never be subject to any outside influence. Whatever your environment is, don't allow your inner peace to be touched by it.

❖ ❖ ❖

When you have mastery of your feelings you abide in your true state. The true state of the Self, the soul, is bliss, wisdom, love, peace. It is to be so happy that no matter what you are doing you enjoy it. Isn't that much better than to blunder through the world like a restless demon, unable to find satisfaction in anything? When centered in your true self, you do every task and enjoy all good things with the joy of God. Filled with His intoxicating bliss, you joyfully perform all actions.

❖ ❖ ❖

In the spiritual life one becomes just like a little child—without resentment, without attachment, full of life and joy.

❖ ❖ ❖

Real happiness can stand the challenge of all outer experiences. When you can bear the crucifixions of others' wrongs against you and still return love and forgiveness; and when you can keep that divine inner peace intact despite all painful thrusts of outer circumstance, then you shall know this happiness.

❖ ❖ ❖

Be silent and calm [in meditation] every night for at least half an hour, preferably much longer, before you retire, and again in the morning before starting the day's activity. This will produce an undaunted, unbreakable inner habit of happiness that will make you able to meet all the trying situations of the everyday battle of life. With that unchangeable happiness within, go about seeking to fulfill the demands of your daily needs.

❖ ❖ ❖

If you keep the eyes of your concentration closed, you cannot see the sun of happiness burning within your bosom; but no matter how tightly you close the eyes of your attention, the fact nevertheless remains that the happiness rays are ever trying to pierce the closed doors of your mind. Open the windows of calmness and you will find a sudden burst of the bright sun of joy within your very Self.

❖ ❖ ❖

The joyous rays of the soul may be perceived if you interiorize your attention. These perceptions may be had by training your mind to enjoy the beautiful scenery of thoughts in the invisible, intangible kingdom within you. Do not search for happiness only in beautiful clothes, clean houses, delicious dinners, soft cushions, and luxuries. These will imprison your happiness behind the bars of externality, of outwardness.

❖ ❖ ❖

I appreciate whatever God gives me, but I don't miss it when it is gone. Someone once gave me a beautiful coat and hat, an expensive outfit. Then began my worry. I had to be concerned about not tearing or soiling it. It made me uncomfortable. I said, "Lord, why did You give me this bother?" One day I was to lecture in Trinity Hall here in Los Angeles. When I arrived at the hall and started to remove my coat, the Lord told me, "Take away your belongings from the pockets." I did so. When I returned to the cloakroom after my lecture, the coat was gone. I was angry, and someone said, "Never mind, we will get you another coat." I replied, "I am not angry because I lost the coat, but because whoever took it didn't take the hat that matches it, too!"

Don't let your feelings rule you. How can you be happy if you are all the time fussing about your clothes or other possessions? Dress neatly in clean clothes and then forget about them; clean your house and forget it.

❖ ❖ ❖

The more you depend upon conditions outside yourself for happiness, the less happiness you will experience.

❖ ❖ ❖

If you think that you can live happily in forgetfulness of God, you are mistaken, because you will cry out in loneliness again and again until you realize that God is all in all—the only reality in the universe. You are made in His image. You can never find lasting happiness in any *thing* because nothing is complete except God.

❖ ❖ ❖

The unalloyed happiness I find in communion with the Lord no words can describe. Night and day I am in a state of joy. That joy is God. To know Him is to perform the funeral rites for all your sorrows. He does not require you to be stoic and morose. This is not the right concept of God, nor the way to please Him. Without being happy you will not even be able to find Him....The happier you are, the greater will be your attunement with Him. Those who know Him are always happy, because God is joy itself.

Affirmations

Beginning with the early dawn, I will radiate my cheer to everyone I meet today. I will be the mental sunshine for all who cross my path this day.

❖ ❖ ❖

I form new habits of thinking by seeing the good everywhere, and by beholding all things as the perfect idea of God made manifest.

❖ ❖ ❖

I will make up my mind to be happy within myself right now, where I am today.

CHAPTER 11

Getting Along With Others

The greatest of all happiness, next to divine happiness, is to be at peace with one's immediate relations, those with whom one must live every day in the year. When people try to handle the extremely complicated machinery of human feelings without any training whatsoever, the consequent results are often disastrous. Very few persons realize that most of our happiness lies in the art of understanding the law of human behavior. That is why so many people are often "in hot water" with their friends, and, worse yet, at constant war with their own best beloved ones at home.

Dealing With Inharmonious Relationships

The basic law of right human behavior is self-reform....Whenever any trouble occurs with our friends or dear ones, we should inwardly lay the blame on ourselves for getting into an unpleasant situation and then try to get out of it as fast and as graciously as we can. It is fruitless to increase the trouble by loudly, unkindly, discourteously blaming others, even though we find that they are to blame. We can teach quick-tempered dear ones to mend their faults a hundred times better by setting a good example than we can by harsh or self-righteous words.

❖ ❖ ❖

When there is a fight, at least two parties are involved. So there can be no fight with you if you refuse to participate.

❖ ❖ ❖

If someone speaks to you in hurtful language, remain quiet; or say, "I am sorry if I have done something to offend you," and then remain silent.

❖ ❖ ❖

The spiritual man conquers wrath by calmness, stops quarrels by keeping silence, dispels inharmony by being sweet of speech, and shames discourtesy by being thoughtful of others.

❖ ❖ ❖

There is no more liberating action than sincerely to give people kindness in return for unkindness.

❖ ❖ ❖

Never be mean. Have resentment toward none. I prefer some sinners with good hearts to some so-called good people who are bigoted and uncompassionate. To be spiritual is to be broad, to understand and forgive, and to be a friend to all.

❖ ❖ ❖

The entire Roman government could not have roused unkindness in Christ. Even for those who crucified him, he prayed: "Father, forgive them; for they know not what they do."*

❖ ❖ ❖

Inward civility, inner heartfelt courtesy, and continuous goodwill are the proper panaceas for all bad behavior.

❖ ❖ ❖

Most of the time, people talk and act from their own viewpoint. They seldom see, or even try to see, the other person's side. If, lacking understanding, you enter into a fight with someone, remember that each of you is as much to blame as the other, regardless of which one started the argument. "Fools argue; wise men discuss."

❖ ❖ ❖

To have calm feeling doesn't mean that you always smile and agree with everyone no matter what they say—that you regard truth but don't want to annoy anybody with it. This is going to the extreme. Those who try in this way to please everyone, with the desire of getting praise for their good nature, do not necessarily have control of feeling....Whoever has control of feeling follows truth, shares that truth wherever he can, and avoids annoying unnecessarily anyone who would not be receptive anyway. He knows when to speak and when to be silent, but he

* Luke 23:34.

...promises his own ideals and inner peace. Such a man is a force for great good in this world.

❖ ❖ ❖

We should make ourselves attractive by wearing the fine garment of genuinely courteous language. We should first of all be courteous to our immediate relatives. When one can do that, he will be habitually kind to all people. Real family happiness has its foundation on the altar of understanding and kind words. It is not necessary to agree on everything in order to show kindness. Calm silence, sincerity, and courteous words, whether one is agreeing or disagreeing with others, mark the person who knows how to behave.

❖ ❖ ❖

If you want to be loved, start loving others who need your love....If you want others to sympathize with you, start showing sympathy to those around you. If you want to be respected, you must learn to be respectful to everyone, both young and old.... Whatever you want others to be, first be that yourself; then you will find others responding in like manner to you.

Developing a Harmonious Personality

Be genuinely amiable when you are with others. Never be a "sourpuss." You don't have to laugh boisterously, like a hyena, but don't wear a long face either. Just be smiling, congenial, and kind. Smiling on the outside when you are angry or resentful inside, however, is hypocrisy. If you want to be likable, be sincere. Sincerity is a soul quality that God has given to every human being, but not all express it. Above all, be humble. Though you may have admirable inner strength, don't overwhelm others with your strong nature. Be calm and considerate of them. This is the way to develop likable magnetism.

❖ ❖ ❖

Don't try to get along with others by adopting artificial mannerisms. Just be loving and ever ready to be helpful and saturate yourself with divine communion—then you will find yourself getting along with everyone in your environment.

❖ ❖ ❖

In your relationships with others, it is extremely necessary to recognize and appreciate the characteristics that they have chiseled out in themselves. If you study people with an open mind, you will better understand them and be able to get along with them. You will instantly be able to tell what kind of person you are dealing with and know how to deal with him. Don't talk to a philosopher about horse racing, or to a scientist about housekeeping. Find out what interests an individual, and then talk with him about that subject, not necessarily what interests you.

❖ ❖ ❖

When you talk, don't talk too much about yourself. Try to speak on a subject that interests the other

. ...d listen. That is the way to be attractive.
You will see how your presence is in demand.

❖ ❖ ❖

An inferiority complex is born of a secret awareness of real or imagined weaknesses. In trying to
compensate for such weaknesses, a person may build
an armor of false pride, and exhibit an inflated ego.
Then those who do not understand the real cause of
such an attitude may say the person has a superiority complex. Both manifestations of his inner inharmony are destructive to Self-development. Both are
fostered by imagination and by ignoring facts, while
neither belongs to the true, all-powerful nature of
the soul. Found your self-confidence upon actual
achievements plus the knowledge that your real Self
(the soul) can never be "inferior" in any way; then
you will be free from all complexes.

❖ ❖ ❖

If the majority find you an unattractive personality, analyze yourself. There may be some traits in
your make-up that are repugnant to others. Perhaps
you talk too much, or you make it a practice to put
your finger into everyone else's pie, or you have the
habit of telling others what is wrong with them and
how they should lead their lives, and you won't accept any suggestions for improving yourself. These
are examples of psychological characteristics that
make us unattractive to others.

❖ ❖ ❖

Consideration for others is a most wonderful quality. It is the greatest attractiveness you can have. Practice it! If someone is thirsty, a thoughtful person anticipates his need and offers him a drink. Consideration means awareness of and attentiveness to others. A considerate person, when in the company of others, will have an intuitive awareness of their needs.

❖ ❖ ❖

Practice consideration and goodness until you are like a beautiful flower that everyone loves to see. Be the beauty that is in a flower, and the attractiveness that is in a pure mind. When you are attractive in that way, you will always have true friends. You will be loved by both man and God.

Overcoming Negative Emotions

Whatever you give out will come back to you. Hate, and you will receive hate in return. When you fill yourself with inharmonious thoughts and emotions, you are destroying yourself. Why hate or be angry with anyone? Love your enemies. Why stew in the heat of anger? If you become riled, get over it at once. Take a walk, count to ten or fifteen, or divert your mind to something pleasant. Let go of the desire to retaliate. When you are angry your brain is overheating, your heart is having valve trouble, your whole body is being devitalized. Exude peace and goodness; because that is the nature of the image of God within you—your true nature. Then no one can disturb you.

❖ ❖ ❖

Whenever you are jealous, you are in collusion with the cosmic delusion of Satan.* Whenever you are angry, Satan is guiding you....Any time the voice of jealousy, fear, or anger speaks, remember that it is not your voice, and command that it be gone. But you will not be able to expel that evil, no matter how you try, so long as you give that negative feeling a safe harbor in your mind. Eradicate jealousy, fear, and anger from within, so that every time an evil impulse tells you to hate and to hurt, another stronger voice within tells you to love and to forgive. Listen to *that* voice.

❖ ❖ ❖

Jealousy comes from an inferiority complex, and expresses itself through suspicion and fear. It signifies that a person is afraid he cannot hold his own in his relationships with others, be they conjugal, filial, social. If you feel you have cause to be jealous of someone—for example, if you are afraid that the one you love is transferring his or her attention to another—first strive to understand if there is something lacking within yourself. Improve yourself; develop yourself. The only way to hold on to the affection or respect of another is to apply the law of love and to merit that recognition by

---

* See *maya* in glossary.

self-improvement....Fulfillment lies in constantly improving yourself so that instead of your seeking others, others will seek you.

❖ ❖ ❖

Even while striving to improve yourself, learn to stand alone, secure in your own virtues and self-worth. If you want others to believe in you, remember, it isn't only your words that have an effect, but what you are and what you feel within—what is in your soul. Always strive to be an angel within, no matter how others behave. Be sincere, kind, loving, and understanding.

❖ ❖ ❖

When someone comes to you in anger, remain in charge of yourself. "I will not lose my temper. I will keep on expressing calmness until his feeling changes."

❖ ❖ ❖

When a loved one...tries our patience beyond endurance, we should retire to a quiet place, lock the door, practice some physical exercise, and then quiet ourselves in the following way:

Sit in a straight chair, with spine erect; slowly inhale and exhale, twelve times. Then deeply affirm mentally, ten times or more: "Father, Thou art harmony. Let me reflect Thy harmony. Harmonize my error-stricken dear one."

One should affirm this until he feels, through the deep sense of peace and calm assurance falling upon him, that God has heard him and has answered.

❖ ❖ ❖

"Aren't your teachings about controlling the emotions dangerous?" a student asked. "Many psychologists claim that suppression leads to mental maladjustments and even to physical illness."

Paramahansa Yogananda replied: "Suppression is harmful—holding the thought that you want something but doing nothing constructive to get it. Self-control is beneficial—patiently replacing wrong thoughts by right ones, changing reprehensible actions to helpful ones.

"Those who dwell on evil hurt themselves. Men who fill their minds with wisdom and their lives with constructive activities spare themselves ignoble suffering."

❖ ❖ ❖

"Wrath springs only from thwarted desires," [Sri Yukteswar said]. "I do not expect anything from others, so their actions cannot be in opposition to wishes of mine."

❖ ❖ ❖

If someone hurts you deeply, you remember it. But instead of concentrating on that, you should think of all the good things about the person who has hurt you, and of all the goodness that you have in your life. Don't take notice of the insults people give you.

❖ ❖ ❖

Concentrate on trying to behold God in your

enemy; for by doing so you release yourself from evil vengeful desires that destroy your peace of mind. By heaping hatred upon hatred, or giving hate in return for hate, you not only increase your enemy's hostility toward you; you poison your system, physically as well as emotionally, with your own venom.

❖ ❖ ❖

Have only love in your heart for others. The more you see the good in them, the more you will establish good in yourself. Hold the consciousness of good. The way to make people good is to see the good in them. Do not nag them. Remain calm, serene, always in command of yourself. You will then find out how easy it is to get along.

❖ ❖ ❖

Cleanse your mind of all adverse criticism of others. Use a look or a hint to correct lovingly a receptive person, but do not force correction, and do not continue to hold critical thoughts, even though you remain silent.

❖ ❖ ❖

Thoughts can sometimes be more effective than words. The human mind is the most powerful broadcasting machine there is. If you constantly broadcast positive thoughts with love, those thoughts will have an effect on others. (Similarly, if you broadcast jealousy or hatred, others receive those thoughts and respond accordingly.) Ask God to put His power behind your efforts. If, for instance, it is the husband that is going astray, the wife should pray to God: "Lord, help me to help my husband. Keep all taint of jealousy and resentment out of my heart. I only pray that he realize his error and change. Lord, be with him; and bless me that I do my part." If your communion with God is deep, you will see that person change.

❖ ❖ ❖

It is easy to strike back, but to give love is the highest way to try to disarm your persecutor. Even if it doesn't work at the time, he will never be able to forget that when he gave you a slap, you gave love in return. That love must be sincere; when it comes from the heart, love is magical. You should not look for the effects; even if your love is spurned, pay no attention. Give love and forget. Don't expect anything; then you will see the magical result.

Forgiveness

The God of some scriptures is a revengeful deity, always ready to punish us. But Jesus showed us the real nature of God....He did not destroy his enemies with "twelve legions of angels,"* but rather overcame evil with the power of divine love. His actions demonstrated the supreme love of God, and the behavior of those who are one with Him.

---

* "Thinkest thou that I cannot now pray to my Father, and he shall presently give me more than twelve legions of angels?" (Matthew 26:53).

❖ ❖ ❖

"One should forgive, under any injury," says the *Mahabharata.** "It hath been said that the continuation of the species is due to man's being forgiving. Forgiveness is holiness; by forgiveness the universe is held together. Forgiveness is the might of the mighty; forgiveness is sacrifice; forgiveness is quiet of mind. Forgiveness and gentleness are the qualities of the Self-possessed. They represent eternal virtue."

❖ ❖ ❖

"Then came Peter to him and said, Lord, how oft shall my brother sin against me, and I forgive him? till seven times? Jesus saith unto him, I say not unto thee, Until seven times: but, Until seventy times seven."† I prayed deeply to understand this uncompromising counsel. "Lord," I protested, "is it possible?" When the Divine Voice finally responded, It brought a humbling flood of light: "How many times, O Man, do I forgive each of you daily?"

❖ ❖ ❖

In your heart must well that sympathy which soothes away all pains from the hearts of others, that sympathy which enabled Jesus to say "Father, forgive them; for they know not what they do."‡ His great love encompassed all. He could have destroyed his

---

* A great epic scripture of India, of which the Bhagavad Gita is a part.

† Matthew 18:21–22.

‡ Luke 23:34.

enemies with a look, yet just as God is constantly forgiving us even though He knows all our wicked thoughts, so those great souls who are in tune with Him give us that same love.

❖ ❖ ❖

If you would develop Christ consciousness,[*] learn to be sympathetic. When genuine feeling for others comes into your heart, you are beginning to manifest that great consciousness….Lord Krishna said: "He is a supreme yogi who regards with equal-mindedness all men…."[†]

❖ ❖ ❖

Wrath and hatred accomplish nothing. Love rewards. You may cow down someone, but once that person has risen again, he will try to destroy you. Then how have you conquered him? You have not. The only way to conquer is by love. And where you cannot conquer, just be silent or get away, and pray for him. That is the way you must love. If you practice this in your life, you will have peace beyond understanding.

---

[*] Universal consciousness; oneness with the omnipresence of God. See glossary.
[†] Bhagavad Gita VI:9.

Affirmations

I will try to please everyone by kind, considerate actions, ever striving to remove any misunderstanding knowingly or unknowingly caused by me.

❖ ❖ ❖

Today I forgive all those who have ever offended me. I give my love to all thirsty hearts, both to those who love me and those who do not love me.

CHAPTER 12

Unconditional Love: Perfecting Human Relationships

The world as a whole has forgotten the real meaning of the word *love*. Love has been so abused and crucified by man that very few people know what true love is. Just as oil is present in every part of the olive, so love permeates every part of creation. But to define love is very difficult, for the same reason that words cannot fully describe the flavor of an orange. You have to taste the fruit to know its flavor. So with love.

❖ ❖ ❖

In the universal sense, love is the divine power of attraction in creation that harmonizes, unites, binds together....Those who live in tune with the attractive force of love achieve harmony with nature and their fellow beings, and are attracted to blissful reunion with God.

❖ ❖ ❖

"Ordinary love is selfish, darkly rooted in desires and satisfactions," [Sri Yukteswar said]. "Divine love is without condition, without boundary, without change. The flux of the human heart is gone forever at the transfixing touch of pure love."

❖ ❖ ❖

Many human beings say "I love you" one day and reject you the next. That is not love. One whose heart is filled with the love of God cannot willfully hurt anyone. When you love God without reservation, He fills your heart with His unconditional love for all. That love no human tongue can describe.... The ordinary man is incapable of loving others in this way. Self-centered in the consciousness of "I, me, and mine," he has not yet discovered the omnipresent God who resides in him and in all other beings. To me there is no difference between one person and another; I behold all as soul-reflections of the one God. I can't think of anyone as a stranger, for I know that we are all part of the One Spirit. When you experience the true meaning of religion, which is to know God, you will realize that He is your Self, and that He exists equally and impartially in all beings. Then you will be able to love others as your own Self.*

❖ ❖ ❖

In the consciousness of one who is immersed in the divine love of God, there is no deception, no narrowness of caste or creed, no boundaries of any kind. When you experience that divine love, you will see no difference between flower and beast, between one

---

* "Thou shalt love the Lord thy God with all thy heart, and with all thy soul, and with all thy strength, and with all thy mind; and thy neighbor as thyself" (Luke 10:27).

human being and another. You will commune with all nature, and you will love equally all mankind.

❖ ❖ ❖

Compassion toward all beings is necessary for divine realization, for God Himself is overflowing with this quality. Those with a tender heart can put themselves in the place of others, feel their suffering, and try to alleviate it.[*]

Balancing Feminine and Masculine Qualities

It seems there has always been a rivalry between man and woman. But they are equals; neither one is superior. Be proud of what you are in this life.

❖ ❖ ❖

"In sleep, you do not know whether you are a man or a woman," [Sri Yukteswar said]. "Just as a man, impersonating a woman, does not become one, so the soul, impersonating both man and woman, remains changeless. The soul is the immutable, unqualified image of God."

❖ ❖ ❖

Do not even allow yourself to be limited to the consciousness that you are a man or a woman:

---

[*] Lord Krishna taught: "The best type of yogi is he who feels for others, whether in grief or pleasure, even as he feels for himself" (Bhagavad Gita VI:32).

You are a soul made in God's image....The wisest course is to remember always, "I am neither man nor woman; I am Spirit." Then you will rid yourself of the limiting consciousness of both tendencies; you will realize your highest divine potential, whether you are incarnate as a man or a woman.

❖ ❖ ❖

God is both infinite wisdom and infinite feeling. When He manifested Himself in creation, God gave His wisdom a form in the father; and He gave His feeling a form in the mother....Every father and every mother is potentially endowed with both the fatherly wisdom and the motherly tenderness of God. They have to perfect these endowments....The divine man develops both the fatherly and motherly qualities in himself.

❖ ❖ ❖

Man argues that woman is emotional and cannot reason; and woman complains that man cannot feel. Both are incorrect. Woman can reason, but feeling is uppermost in her nature; and man can feel, but in him reason is predominant.

❖ ❖ ❖

God created these physiological and mental differences in order to make some distinction between man and woman. The ideal spiritual union between them was meant to bring out the hidden feeling in man and to develop the hidden reason in woman.

They were meant to aid each other in developing the pure divine qualities of perfect reason and feeling.

❖ ❖ ❖

Each sex should strive toward a balance by learning from one another through friendship and understanding.

❖ ❖ ❖

Unless man and woman understand each other's nature, they ignorantly torture one another....Each should strive for an inner balance of both reason and feeling, and so become a "whole" personality, a perfected human being.

❖ ❖ ❖

By God-communion you bring about the harmony or balance of these two qualities within yourself.

❖ ❖ ❖

In the great saints we see combined the ideal masculine and feminine qualities. Jesus was like that; so were all the masters. When you have attained that perfect reason-feeling equilibrium, you will have learned one of the major lessons for which you were sent here.

❖ ❖ ❖

Mankind must realize that the basic nature of the soul is spiritual. For man and woman to look upon each other only as a means to satisfy lust is to court the destruction of happiness. Slowly, bit by bit, peace of mind will go.

❖ ❖ ❖

Man should strive to see the God in woman, and to help her realize her spiritual nature. He should make her feel that she is with him not merely to satisfy his sensual appetite, but as a companion whom he respects and regards as an expression of the Divine. And woman should look upon man in the same way.

❖ ❖ ❖

When man and woman genuinely and purely love one another, there is complete harmony between them in body, mind, and soul. When their love is expressed in its highest form, it results in a perfect unity.

Marriage

Two persons who unite their lives to help each other toward divine realization are founding their marriage on the right basis: unconditional friendship.

❖ ❖ ❖

To develop pure and unconditional love between husband and wife, parent and child, friend and friend, self and all, is the lesson we have come on earth to learn.

❖ ❖ ❖

True marriage is a laboratory in which poisons of selfishness, bad temper, and bad behavior may be poured into the test tube of patience and neutralized and changed by the catalytic power of love and constant effort to behave nobly.

❖ ❖ ❖

If there is a habit or quality in your mate that rouses unlovely traits in your disposition, you should realize the purpose of this circumstance: to bring to the surface those poisons hidden within you so that you may eliminate them and thus purify your nature.

❖ ❖ ❖

The greatest thing a husband or wife can wish for the spouse is spirituality; for soul unfoldment brings out the divine qualities of understanding, patience, thoughtfulness, love. But each should remember that the desire for spiritual growth cannot be forced on the other. Live love yourself, and your goodness will inspire all your loved ones.

❖ ❖ ❖

Unless married couples keep in mind the true high purpose of marriage, they may never enjoy a really happy life together. Oversexuality, too much familiarity, lack of courtesy, suspiciousness, insulting speech or acts, arguing before children or guests, crankiness, and unloading of troubles or anger on one's mate should be disallowed if marriage is to be ideal.

❖ ❖ ❖

The *first* and most essential requirement for a

happy marriage is soul unity—similarity of spiritual ideals and goals, implemented by a practical willingness to attain those goals by study, effort, and self-discipline. Couples who possess soul unity will be able to make a success of marriage even if no other desirable basis is present.

The *second* requirement for a happy marriage is similarity of interest—intellectual, social, environmental, and so on.

The *third*, and last in importance (though usually given first place by unenlightened people), is physical attraction. That bond soon loses its attractive power if the first requirement, or the first and second requirements, are not also present.

❖ ❖ ❖

People who want to marry should first have to learn to control their emotions.* Two people placed together in the arena of marriage without this training battle worse than opponents in a World War! Wars, at least, come to an end after a time; but some marital partners engage in combat throughout life. You would think that in a civilized society people should know how to get along, but few have learned this art. A marriage should be nurtured on high ideals and the wine of God's inspiration; then it will be a happy and mutually beneficial union.

❖ ❖ ❖

* See also pages 141 ff.

If husbands and wives who are accustomed to using each other for target practice, using bullets of wrathful language and discourtesies, would try instead to entertain each other with the soul-solacing charm of kind words, they would then create a new happiness in family life.

❖ ❖ ❖

Sex has its place in the marital relationship between man and woman. But if it becomes the supreme factor in that relationship, love flies out the door and disappears completely; in its place come possessiveness, over-familiarity, and the abuse and loss of friendship and understanding. Though sexual attraction is one of the conditions under which love is born, sex in itself is not love. Sex and love are as far apart as the moon and the sun. It is only when the transmuting quality of true love is uppermost in the relationship that sex becomes a means of expressing love. Those who live too much on the sex plane lose their way and fail to find a satisfying marital relationship. It is by self-control, in which sex is not the ruling emotion, but only incidental to love, that husband and wife can know what real love is. In this modern world, unfortunately, love is too often destroyed by overemphasis on sex experience.

❖ ❖ ❖

Those who practice a natural—not forced—moderation in their sex life develop other enduring qualities in the husband-wife relationship:

friendship, companionship, understanding, mutual love. For example, Madame Amelita Galli-Curci* and her husband, Homer Samuels, are the greatest lovers I have met in the West. Their love is beautiful because they practice these ideals of which I speak. When parted even for a short time, they eagerly look forward to seeing each other again, to being in each other's company, to sharing their thoughts and love.

❖ ❖ ❖

Every individual needs a period of aloneness or solitude in order to cope with the increasing pressures of life....Do not encroach upon one another's independence.

❖ ❖ ❖

When the husband serves the wife, and she serves him, each with the desire to see the other happy, Christ Consciousness—God's loving Cosmic Intelligence that permeates every atom of creation—has begun to express itself through their consciousness.

❖ ❖ ❖

When two people feel an unconditional attraction for each other, and are ready to sacrifice for one another, they are truly in love.

* World-renowned opera singer (1889–1963) who met Paramahansa Yogananda during his early years in the United States. She and her husband became devoted members of Self-Realization Fellowship. Madame Galli-Curci wrote the foreword to Paramahansa Yogananda's book *Whispers from Eternity*.

❖ ❖ ❖

To wish for perfection for the loved one, and to feel pure joy in thinking of that soul, is divine love; and that is the love of true friendship.

❖ ❖ ❖

Meditate together every morning, and especially at night....Have a little family altar where both husband and wife, and children, gather to offer deep devotion unto God and unite their souls forever in ever-joyous Cosmic Consciousness.... *The more you meditate together, the deeper your love for one another will grow.

Friendship

Friendship is God's trumpet call, bidding the soul destroy the partitions of ego-consciousness that separate it from all other souls and from Him.

❖ ❖ ❖

Friendship is the purest form of God's love because it is born of the heart's free choice and is not imposed upon us by familial instinct. Ideal friends never part; nothing can sever their fraternal relationship.

❖ ❖ ❖

The treasure of friendship is your richest possession, because it goes with you beyond this life. All

* See glossary.

the true friends you have made you will meet again in the home of the Father, for real love is never lost.

❖ ❖ ❖

When perfect friendship exists either between two hearts or within a group of hearts in a spiritual relationship, such friendship perfects each individual.

❖ ❖ ❖

There is a magnet in your heart that will attract true friends. That magnet is unselfishness, thinking of others first. Very few persons are free from self-centeredness. Yet one can develop the quality of unselfishness very easily if he practices thinking of others first.

❖ ❖ ❖

You cannot attract true friends without removing from your own character the stains of selfishness and other unlovely qualities. The greatest art of making friends is to behave divinely yourself—to be spiritual, to be pure, to be unselfish....The more your human shortcomings drop away and divine qualities come into your life, the more friends you will have.

❖ ❖ ❖

True friendship consists in being mutually useful in offering one's friend good cheer in distress, sympathy in sorrow, advice in trouble, and material help in times of real need....One who has given his friendship to another gladly foregoes selfish pleasures or self-interest for the sake of his friend's happiness, without consciousness of loss or sacrifice, and without counting the cost.

❖ ❖ ❖

No matter what difference of opinion there is between you and such friends, there is always understanding and communication. In that relationship, regardless of differing views, you have mutual respect and cherish your friendship above everything else. True friendship established in God is the only relationship that is lasting.

❖ ❖ ❖

If you proffer friendship, you must mean it. You must not show kindness or cooperation outside, and inside feel the opposite. Spiritual law is very powerful. Don't go against spiritual principles. Never deceive or be treacherous. As a friend, know when to mind your own business; understand your place; know when you should have the willingness to cooperate, and when you should have the will to noncooperate.

❖ ❖ ❖

It is wrong to speak the truth when, by doing so, one betrays another person unnecessarily and to no good purpose. Suppose a man drinks, but tries to hide it from the rest of the world. You know about his weakness, and so in the name of truthfulness you announce to your friends, "You know that so and so drinks, don't you?" Such a remark is uncalled for;

one should not be busy about other people's business. Be protective about others' personal faults, so long as they harm no one else. Speak privately to an offender about his failings, if you have an opportunity or responsibility to help him; but never, under pretext of helping someone, speak deliberately to hurt him. You will only "help" him to become your enemy. You may also extinguish any desire that he might have had to become better.

❖ ❖ ❖

Help your friend by being a mental, aesthetic, and spiritual inspiration to him. Never be sarcastic to a friend. Do not flatter him unless it is to encourage him. Do not agree with him when he is wrong.

❖ ❖ ❖

Be true, be sincere, and friendship will steadily grow. I remember a discussion with Sri Yukteswar about sincerity. I had said, "Sincerity is everything."

"No," he responded, "sincerity plus thoughtfulness is everything." He went on: "Suppose you are sitting in the parlor in your home, and there is a beautiful new carpet on the floor. It is raining outside. A friend you haven't seen in many years flings open the door and rushes into the room to greet you."

"That is all right," I said. But my Guru had yet to make his point.

"You were sincerely happy to see each other," he said, "but wouldn't you have liked it better if he had been thoughtful enough to take off his muddy boots before he came in and ruined the carpet?"

I had to agree he was right.

No matter how well you think of someone, or how close you are to that person, it is important to sweeten that relationship with good manners and thoughtfulness. Then friendship becomes truly wonderful and enduring. Familiarity that leads you to be inconsiderate is very harmful to friendship.

❖ ❖ ❖

Just as dew helps the flower to grow, so inner and outer sweetness fosters the growth of friendship.

❖ ❖ ❖

Friendship is noble, fruitful, holy—
When two separate souls march in difference
Yet in harmony; agreeing and disagreeing,
Glowingly improving diversely....
Ah, friendship—flowering, heaven-born plant!
Nurtured art thou in the soil of measureless love,
In the seeking of soul progress together
By two who would smooth the way, each for the
    other.*

❖ ❖ ❖

To be a true, unconditional friend, your love must be anchored in God's love. Your life with God is the inspiration behind true divine friendship with all.

* From the poem "Friendship," in *Songs of the Soul* by Paramahansa Yogananda.

❖ ❖ ❖

Try to perfect your friendship with a few souls. When you can truly give unconditional friendship to them, then your heart will be ready to give perfect friendship to all. And when you can do that, you become divine—like God and the great ones, who give friendship to every being, irrespective of personality. Friendship that remains centered on only one or two souls, to the exclusion of others, is like a river that loses itself in the sands, never reaching the ocean. The river of divine friendship broadens as it flows onward, powerful and truthful, eventually merging in the oceanic presence of God.

Affirmation

As I radiate love and goodwill to others, I will open the channel for God's love to come to me. Divine love is the magnet that draws to me all good.

CHAPTER 13

Understanding Death

Though the ordinary man looks upon death with dread and sadness, those who have gone before know it as a wondrous experience of peace and freedom.

❖ ❖ ❖

Perhaps we wonder most of all about those we love. Where are they? Why are they spirited away from us? A brief good-bye, and then they disappear behind the veil of death. We feel so helpless and sad; and there is nothing we can do about it....When someone is dying, though he cannot speak, a desire is expressed in his consciousness. He is thinking, "I am leaving my loved ones; will I ever see them again?" And those whom he is leaving behind also think, "I am losing him. Will he remember me? Will we meet again?"...When I lost my mother in this life, I promised myself that I would never again be attached to anyone.* I gave my love to God. That first experience with death was very serious for me. But through it I learned much. I searched undaunted for months and years until I found the answer to the

---

* Paramahansa Yogananda was only eleven years old when his mother died. He stormed the very gates of heaven with his youthful spiritual determination until he experienced response from God and the realization that it is God's love expressing through the forms of all our loved ones. To love God is to love all without exclusiveness or the inevitable pain associated with attachment. *(Publisher's Note)*

mystery of life and death....What I tell you, I have experienced.

❖ ❖ ❖

At death, you forget all the limitations of the physical body and realize how free you are. For the first few seconds there is a sense of fear—fear of the unknown, of something unfamiliar to the consciousness. But after that comes a great realization: the soul feels a joyous sense of relief and freedom. You know that you exist apart from the mortal body.

❖ ❖ ❖

Every one of us is going to die someday, so there is no use in being afraid of death. You don't feel miserable at the prospect of losing consciousness of your body in sleep; you accept sleep as a state of freedom to look forward to. So is death; it is a state of rest, a pension from this life. There is nothing to fear. When death comes, laugh at it. Death is only an experience through which you are meant to learn a great lesson: you cannot die.

❖ ❖ ❖

Our real self, the soul, is immortal. We may sleep for a little while in that change called death, but we can never be destroyed. We exist, and that existence is eternal. The wave comes to the shore, and then goes back to the sea; it is not lost. It becomes one with the ocean, or returns again in the form of another wave.* This body has come, and it will vanish; but the soul essence within it will never cease to exist. Nothing can terminate that eternal consciousness.

❖ ❖ ❖

Even a particle of matter or a wave of energy is indestructible, as science has proved; the soul or spiritual essence of man is also indestructible. Matter undergoes change; the soul undergoes changing experiences. Radical changes are termed death, but death or a change in form does not change or destroy the spiritual essence.

❖ ❖ ❖

The body is only a garment. How many times you have changed your clothing in this life, yet because of this you would not say that *you* have changed. Similarly, when you give up this bodily dress at death you do not change. You are just the same, an immortal soul, a child of God.

❖ ❖ ❖

The word "death" is a great misnomer, for there is no death; when you are tired of life, you simply take off the overcoat of flesh and go back to the astral world.†

❖ ❖ ❖

* A reference to reincarnation. See glossary.

† Heaven, the subtle region of higher forces and consciousness. See *astral world* in glossary.

The Bhagavad Gita* speaks beautifully and so-lacingly of the immortality of the soul:

> Never the spirit was born; the spirit shall cease
>   to be never;
> Never was time it was not; End and Beginning
>   are dreams!
> Birthless and deathless and changeless remaineth
>   the spirit forever;
> Death hath not touched it at all, dead though the
>   house of it seems!

❖ ❖ ❖

Death is not the end: it is temporary emancipation, given to you when karma, the law of justice, determines that your present body and environment have served their purpose, or when you are too weary or exhausted by suffering to bear the burden of physical existence any longer. To those who are suffering, death is resurrection from the painful tortures of flesh into awakened peace and calmness. To the elderly, it is a pension earned by years of struggling through life. For all, it is a welcome rest.

❖ ❖ ❖

When you reflect that this world is filled with death, and that your body, too, has to be relinquished, God's plan seems very cruel. You can't imagine that He is merciful. But when you look at the process of death with the eye of wisdom, you see that after all it is merely a thought of God passing through a

---

* II:20, Sir Edwin Arnold's translation.

nightmare of change into blissful freedom in Him
again. Saint and sinner alike are given freedom at
death, to a greater or lesser degree according to merit.
In the Lord's dream astral world—the land to which
souls go at death—they enjoy a freedom such as they
never knew during their earthly life. So don't pity
the person who is passing through the delusion of
death, for in a little while he will be free. Once he
gets out of that delusion, he sees that death was not
so bad after all. He realizes his mortality was only a
dream and rejoices that now no fire can burn him, no
water can drown him; he is free and safe.*

❖ ❖ ❖

The consciousness of the dying man finds itself
suddenly relieved of the weight of the body, of the necessity to breathe, and of any physical pain. A sense
of soaring through a tunnel of very peaceful, hazy,
dim light is experienced by the soul. Then the soul
drifts into a state of oblivious sleep, a million times
deeper and more enjoyable than the deepest sleep
experienced in the physical body....The after-death
state is variously experienced by different people
in accordance with their modes of living while on
earth. Just as different people vary in the duration

---

* "No weapon can pierce the soul; no fire can burn it; no water can
moisten it; nor can any wind wither it....The soul is immutable,
all-permeating, ever calm, and immovable—eternally the same. The
soul is said to be imponderable, unmanifested, and unchangeable.
Therefore, knowing it to be such, thou shouldst not lament" (Bhagavad Gita II:23–25).

and depth of their sleep, so do they vary in their experiences after death. The good man who works hard in the factory of life goes into a deep, unconscious, restful sleep for a short while. He then awakens in some region of life in the astral world: "In my Father's house are many mansions."*

❖ ❖ ❖

"I have never been able to believe in heaven," a new student remarked. "Is there truly such a place?"

"Yes," Paramahansa Yogananda replied. "Those who love God and put their trust in Him go there when they die. On that astral plane, one has power to materialize anything immediately by sheer thought. The astral body is made of shimmering light. In those realms colors and sounds exist that earth knows nothing about. It is a beautiful and enjoyable world."

❖ ❖ ❖

[Death] is not the end of things, but a transfer from physical experiences in the gross domain of changeable matter to purer joys in the astral realm of multicolored lights.

❖ ❖ ❖

"The astral world is infinitely beautiful, clean, pure, and orderly," [Sri Yukteswar said]. "There are no dead planets or barren lands. The terrestrial blemishes—weeds, bacteria, insects, snakes—are absent. Unlike the variable climates and seasons of

---

* John 14:2.

the earth, the astral planets maintain the even temperature of an eternal spring, with occasional luminous white snow and rain of many-colored lights. Astral planets abound in opal lakes and bright seas and rainbow rivers."

❖ ❖ ❖

Souls in the astral region are clothed in gossamer light. They do not encase themselves in bundles of bones with fleshly covers. They carry no frail, heavy frames that collide with other crude solids and break. Therefore, there is no war in the astral land between man's body and solids, oceans, lightning, and disease. Nor are there accidents, for all things coexist in mutual helpfulness, rather than antagonism. All forms of vibration function in harmony with one another. All forces live in peace and conscious helpfulness. The souls, the rays on which they tread, and the orange rays they drink and eat, all are made of living light. Souls live in mutual cognizance and cooperation, breathing not oxygen, but the joy of Spirit.

❖ ❖ ❖

"Friends of other lives easily recognize one another in the astral world," [Sri Yukteswar said]. "Rejoicing at the immortality of friendship, they realize the indestructibility of love, often doubted at the time of the sad, delusive partings of earthly life."

❖ ❖ ❖

Why do we cry when our dear ones die? Because we sorrow for our own loss. If our loved ones leave us for training in better schools of life, we should rejoice instead of being selfishly sad, for we may keep them earthbound and hamper their progress by broadcasting our own selfish wills. The Lord is ever new, and by His infinite magic wand, Renewing Death, He keeps each created object, each living being, ever manifesting, ever remodeling itself into a fitter vehicle for His inexhaustible expressions. Death comes to dutiful men as a promotion to a higher state; it comes to failures to give them another chance in a different environment.

❖ ❖ ❖

Death is the culmination of life. In death life seeks rest. It is precursor to the greatest happiness, the exquisite freedom from all tortures of flesh. Death automatically dismisses all bodily pain, just as sleep banishes the weariness and aches of the hard-worked body. Death is a parole from the prison of the physical body.

❖ ❖ ❖

The ignorant man sees only the unsurmountable wall of death, hiding, seemingly forever, his cherished friends. But the man of unattachment, he who loves others as expressions of the Lord, understands that at death the dear ones have only returned for a breathing space of joy in Him.

❖ ❖ ❖

How glorious is life after death! No more will you have to lug about this old baggage of bones, with all its troubles. You will be free in the astral heaven, unhindered by physical limitations.

❖ ❖ ❖

I once wrote about a vision I had of a dying youth, in which God showed me the right attitude toward death. The youth was lying in bed and was told by his doctors that he had just one day to live. He replied, "One day to reach my Beloved! when death shall open the gates of immortality and I shall be free from the prison bars of pain. Don't cry for me, ye who are left on this desolate shore, still to mourn and deplore; it is I who pity you. You weep for me dark tears, crying for your loss in me; but I weep for you joyous tears, because I am going before you, for your welfare's sake, to light candles of wisdom all the way. And I shall wait to welcome you there where I shall be, with my only Beloved and yours. O dear ones, rejoice in my joy!"*

❖ ❖ ❖

You don't know what is going to come to you in this world; you have to go on living and worrying. Those who die are pitying us; they are blessing us. Why should you grieve for them? I told this [story of the dying youth] to a woman who had lost her son. When I finished explaining, she dried her tears immediately and said, "Never before have I felt

---

* Paramahansa Yogananda here paraphrases his poem, "The Dying Youth's Divine Reply," from *Songs of the Soul*.

such peace. I am glad to know that my son is free. I thought something awful had happened to him."

❖ ❖ ❖

When a dear one dies, instead of grieving unreasonably, realize that he has gone on to a higher plane at the will of God, and that God knows what is best for him. Rejoice that he is free. Pray that your love and goodwill be messengers of encouragement to him on his forward path. This attitude is much more helpful. Of course, we would not be human if we did not miss loved ones; but in feeling lonesome for them we don't want selfish attachment to be the cause of keeping them earthbound. Extreme sorrow prevents a departed soul from going ahead toward greater peace and freedom.

❖ ❖ ❖

[There is a right kind of sorrow in the face of death, as expressed by Paramahansa Yogananda in the memorial service he conducted for Sri Gyanamata, one of his earliest and foremost disciples, whom he lovingly and respectfully referred to as "Sister." *]*

Someone said to me last night, when there were tears in my eyes, that I should be happy that Sister is free in the joy of Spirit. I said, "I know all that, how happy Sister is, how this glorious chapter of her life is closed, how the pain is gone from her body....My

---

* See page 47.

spirit is with hers in God. But these are tears of love, that on this side I shall miss her...."

That bright and humble light that was Sister was extinguished before me, and has commingled with the Great Light. That is my contentment, and my sadness. And I am glad to be sad, glad that she was with us to inspire so much love from our hearts.

❖ ❖ ❖

To send your thoughts to loved ones who have passed on, sit quietly in your room and meditate upon God. When you feel His peace within you, concentrate deeply at the Christ center,* the center of will at the point between the two eyebrows, and broadcast your love to those dear ones who are gone. Visualize at the Christ center the person you wish to contact. Send to that soul your vibrations of love, and of strength and courage. If you do this continuously, and if you don't lose the intensity of your interest in that loved one, that soul will definitely receive your vibrations. Such thoughts give your loved ones a sense of well-being, a sense of being loved. They have not forgotten you any more than you have forgotten them.

❖ ❖ ❖

Send your thoughts of love and goodwill to your loved ones as often as you feel inclined to do so, but at least once a year—perhaps on some special

---

* See glossary.

anniversary. Mentally tell them, "We will meet again sometime and continue to develop our divine love and friendship with one another." If you send them your loving thoughts continuously now, someday you will surely meet them again. You will know that this life is not the end, but merely one link in the eternal chain of your relationship with your loved ones.

Affirmations

O Divine Mother, whether I float on the surface of the present life or sink beneath the waves of death, I rest on the sea bosom of Thy protecting, omnipresent eternal life; I am held in Thine immortal arms.

❖ ❖ ❖

From star to star I will fly; whether on this side of eternity, or the other side of eternity, or whether surging through the waves of life, from atom to atom—flying with the lights, whirling with the stars, or dancing with human lives! I am an immortal! I have resurrected myself from the consciousness of death.

❖ ❖ ❖

The eternal life of God flows through me. I am immortal. Behind the wave of my mind is the ocean of Cosmic Consciousness.

CHAPTER 14

How to Use Thoughts of Immortality to Awaken Your True Self

[Paramahansa Yogananda wrote:

"If you tune in with the thought of God and hit the nail of delusion with the hammer of right thoughts of Truth, you can overcome delusion. Destroy all mortal thoughts by substituting a thought of immortality."

Highlighted in this compilation from his talks and writings are affirmations and soul perceptions—"thoughts of immortality"—that you can use for a greater awareness of the Eternal, Blissful Reality within yourself and pervading all creation.]

Day and Night, Affirm What You Really Are

Unceasingly repeat to yourself this truth:

"I am the Changeless, I am the Infinite. I am not a little mortal being with bones to break, a body that will perish. I am the deathless, changeless Infinite."

❖ ❖ ❖

If a drunken prince goes into the slums and,

forgetting entirely his true identity, begins lamenting, "How poor I am," his friends will laugh at him and say, "Wake up, and remember that you are a prince." You have been likewise in a state of hallucination, thinking you are a helpless mortal, struggling and miserable. Every day you should sit quietly and affirm, with deep conviction:

"No birth, no death, no caste have I; father, mother, have I none. Blessed Spirit, I am He. I am the Infinite Happiness."

If you again and again repeat these thoughts, day and night, you will eventually realize what you really are: an immortal soul.

Peel Away All Limiting Thoughts That Hide Your True Self

Isn't it strange that you do not know who you are? that you do not know your own Self? You define yourself by so many different titles applicable to your body and mortal roles....You must peel off these titles from the soul.

"I think, but I am not the thought. I feel, but I am not the feeling. I will, but I am not the will."

What is left? The you that knows you exist; the you that feels you exist—through the proof given by intuition, the soul's unconditioned knowing of its own existence.

❖ ❖ ❖

Throughout the day, you are constantly working through the body, and so you become identified with it. But every night God removes from you that imprisoning delusion. Last night in deep dreamless sleep, were you a woman or a man or an American or Hindu or rich or poor? No. You were pure Spirit.... In the semi-superconscious freedom of deep sleep God takes away all your mortal titles and makes you feel that you are apart from the body and all its limitations—pure consciousness, resting in space. That vastness is your real Self.

❖ ❖ ❖

Remind yourself of this truth each morning as you awaken:

"I am just coming from the inner perception of my Self. I am not the body. I am invisible. I am Joy. I am Light. I am Wisdom. I am Love. I dwell in the dream body through which I am dreaming this earth life; but I am ever eternal Spirit."

Know Your Self as Inseparable From God

The highest wisdom is Self-realization—knowing the Self, the soul, as eternally inseparable from God....The One Being is at the innermost core of all that exists. "O Arjuna! I am the Self in the heart of all creatures: I am their Origin, Existence, and Finality."

❖ ❖ ❖

All great teachers declare that within this body
is the immortal soul, a spark of That which sustains
all. He who knows his soul knows this truth:

> *"I am beyond everything finite....I am the
> stars, I am the waves, I am the Life of all; I
> am the laughter within all hearts, I am the
> smile on the faces of flowers and in each soul.
> I am the Wisdom and Power that sustain all
> creation."*

Think, Affirm, Realize Your Divine Nature

Destroy the wrong thought of ages—that we are
frail human beings. We must think, meditate, affirm,
believe and realize daily that we are sons of God.

❖ ❖ ❖

You may say, "That is only a thought." Well,
what is thought? Everything you see is the result
of an idea....Invisible thought gives all things their
reality. Therefore if you can control your thought
processes, you can make anything visible; you can
materialize it by the power of your concentration....

Learning to control your thoughts and interiorize
your mind, by scientific guru-given techniques of
meditation, you will gradually develop spiritually:
your meditations will deepen and your invisible self,

the soul-image of God within, will become real to you.

❖ ❖ ❖

Think away the thoughts you want to destroy, by replacing them with constructive thoughts. This is the key to heaven; it is in your hands....

We are what we *think* we are....Change your consciousness from that of a mortal to a divine being.

❖ ❖ ❖

"I am infinite. I am spaceless, I am timeless; I am beyond body, thought, and utterance; beyond all matter and mind. I am endless bliss."

Constantly Impress the Mind With Divine Truth

Avoid any suggestion to the mind of human limitation: sickness, old age, death. Instead, constantly impress the mind with this truth:

"I am the Infinite that has become the body. The body as a manifestation of Spirit is the ever-perfect, ever-youthful Spirit."

❖ ❖ ❖

Refuse to be limited by thoughts of weakness or age. Who told you that you are old? You are not old. You, the soul, are eternally young. Impress that thought on your consciousness:

"I am the soul, a reflection of ever-youthful

Spirit. I am vibrant with youth, with ambition, with power to succeed."

❖ ❖ ❖

Attune yourself to Cosmic Power, and whether you are working in a factory, or mixing with people in the business world, always affirm:

"Within me is the Infinite Creative Power. I shall not go to the grave without some accomplishments. I am a God-man, a rational creature. I am the power of Spirit, the dynamic Source of my soul. I shall create revelations in the world of business, in the world of thought, in the world of wisdom. I and my Father are One. I can create anything I desire, even as my creative Father."

❖ ❖ ❖

[The] *SRF Lessons* teach you how to contact Cosmic Life...the ocean of God's cosmic energy. The greatest method is to tap that energy directly from the inner source and not through the artificial stimuli of medicines, emotion, and so on. Then you can say:

"Right beneath the flesh is a tremendous current. I forgot it, but now, by digging with the pickax of Self-realization, I have discovered that life force again....I am not the flesh. I am the charge of divine electricity that permeates this body."

Your Soul Cannot Be Harmed by Trials

Know you are immortal—not to be crushed by mortal lessons, but to learn and manifest your immortality and *smile*. Say:

"I am immortal, sent to a mortal school to learn and regain my immortality. Though challenged by all the purifying fires of the earth, I am the soul and cannot be destroyed. Fire cannot burn me; water cannot wet me; breezes cannot wither me; atoms cannot shatter me; I am the immortal dreaming the lessons of immortality—not to be crushed, but to be entertained."

❖ ❖ ❖

You have played many roles through many incarnations. But they were all given to entertain you—not to frighten you. Your immortal soul cannot be touched. In the motion picture of life you may cry, you may laugh, you may play many parts; but inwardly you should ever say, "I am Spirit." Great consolation comes from realization of that wisdom.

❖ ❖ ❖

"I am the blessed child of sweet Immortality, sent here to play the drama of births and deaths, but always remembering my deathless Self."

"The Ocean of Spirit has become the little bubble of my soul. I am this bubble of life—one

with the ocean of Cosmic Consciousness. I can never die. Whether floating in birth or disappearing in death, I am indestructible consciousness, protected in the bosom of Spirit's immortality."

Fear Nothing, for You Are a Child of God

When you close your eyes in meditation, you see the vastness of your consciousness—you see that you are in the center of eternity. Concentrate there; take a little time in the morning and the evening just to close your eyes and say:

"I am the Infinite; I am His child. The wave is a bulge of the ocean; my consciousness is a bulge of the great Cosmic Consciousness. I am afraid of nothing. I am Spirit."

❖ ❖ ❖

Always hold on to the consciousness of God's underlying presence. Be of even mind, and say:

"I am fearless; I am made of the substance of God. I am a spark of the Fire of Spirit. I am an atom of the Cosmic Flame. I am a cell of the vast universal body of the Father. 'I and my Father are One.'"

❖ ❖ ❖

Be fearless in the consciousness:

"In life and death I am ever living in God."

Day by day this consciousness will impinge on you when you practice the techniques. When you enter the deep interiorized calmness in meditation, you are free from the bondage of the body. Then what is death to you? Where is fear? Nothing has the power to make you afraid. That is the state you are seeking. Concentrate on *Aum*, merge with *Aum* in deep meditation; through realization of God's immanence in Cosmic Vibration, you will "come unto the Father"—the Bliss-Consciousness of the infinite transcendent Absolute. You will say:

> *"I and my Bliss God are One. I have everything in this universe. Death, disease, doomsday, fires, nothing can take that Bliss away!"*

You Are Spirit: Affirm Your Spiritual Qualities

Try to remember and concentrate on all the beautiful and positive qualities of your life, and do not affirm your deficiencies.

❖ ❖ ❖

The aspiring yogi should always bear in mind, when he feels angry, "That is not me!" When his self-possession is being overpowered by lust or greed, he should say to himself, "That is not me!" When hatred tries to obscure his real nature with a mask of ugly emotion, he should forcefully dissociate himself from it: "That is not me!" He learns to shut the doors of his consciousness against all undesirable visitors seeking lodging within. And whenever that devotee has been used or abused by others, and yet he feels within a stirring of the holy spirit of forgiveness and love, he can then affirm with conviction, "*That* is me! That is my real nature."

Yoga meditation is the process of cultivating and stabilizing the awareness of one's real nature, through definite spiritual and psychophysical methods and laws by which the narrow ego, the flawed hereditary human consciousness, is displaced by the consciousness of the soul.

❖ ❖ ❖

Dear ones, let no one call you a sinner. You are sons of God, for He made you in His image....Say to yourself:

> "No matter if my sins be as deep as the ocean and as high as the stars, still I am unconquered, because I am Spirit Itself."

You Are Light, You Are Joy

Darkness may reign in a cave for thousands of years, but bring in the light, and the darkness vanishes as though it had never been. Similarly, no matter what your defects, they are yours no longer when you bring in the light of goodness. So great is the light of the soul that incarnations of evil cannot destroy it. But the self-created temporary darkness of evil makes the soul miserable, because you suffer in that darkness. You can drive it away by opening your spiritual eye in deep meditation, filling your consciousness with its all-revealing divine light.

No one else can save you. You are your own savior as soon as you realize:

"I am Light Itself. Darkness was never meant for me; it can never cover the light of my soul."

❖ ❖ ❖

Forget the nightmare of present limitations. Before sleep at night and on waking at dawn affirm:

"I am a son of God, even as Jesus and the Masters are. I shall not hide from Him behind the curtain of ignorance. I shall sparkle with wisdom, so that I may fully receive His all-perfect light through my ever-increasing spiritual transparency. Receiving His light fully, I shall know myself to be a son of God, which I always was, being made in His image."

❖ ❖ ❖

"I am the child of God evermore. My power is greater than all my tests. What wrong things I did in the past, I can now undo by good actions and meditation. I will destroy them. I am an immortal evermore."

❖ ❖ ❖

Meditate every night until you can banish all your mundane thoughts and desires....Stand aside from all your restless thoughts and feelings and sit in the temple of your soul, wherein the vast joy of

God expands and engulfs this world, and you realize there is naught else but That. Then you will say:

"I am one with the eternal light of God, the eternal joy of Christ. All the waves of creation are tumbling within me. I have dissolved my body-wave in the ocean of Spirit. I am the ocean of Spirit. No longer am I the body. My spirit is sleeping in the stones. I am dreaming in the flowers, and I am singing in the birds. I am thinking in man, and in the superman I know that I am."

In this state you realize that fire cannot destroy you; that earth and grass and sky are all your blood relations. Then like a spirit you walk on earth, no more afraid of the tumultuous waves of creation.

You Are Love

"My Heavenly Father is love, and I am made in His image. I am the sphere of love in which all planets, all stars, all beings, all creation are glimmering. I am the love that pervades the whole universe."

❖ ❖ ❖

When you experience that divine love, you will see no difference between flower and beast, between one human being and another. You will commune with all nature, and you will love equally all mankind. Beholding but one race—the children of God, your brothers and sisters in Him—you will say to yourself:

> *"God is my Father. I am part of His vast family of human beings. I love them, for they are all mine. I love, too, my brother sun and my sister moon, and all creatures my Father has created and in whom His life flows."*

❖ ❖ ❖

> *"I welcome all races—the olive, the white, the dark, yellow, and red—to their home in my bosom to live with me as my brothers, earthborn of common parents, Adam and Eve, and Spirit-born of Father God.*

> *"I embrace the earth, water, fire, air, ether as my blood relations—one common life roaming through my veins in every form that lives. I enfold all animals, plants, beloved atoms, and energies, in the temple of my life; for I am Love, I am life itself."*

"Thou Art That"

Jnana, or true knowledge, is the soul's realization of *"Aham Brahmasmi* (I am Brahma)," or *"Tat tvam asi* (Thou art That)." And when one sits erect in meditation posture and directs the pranic current to the *Kutastha* (between the eyebrows), that is true *tapasya*, spiritual austerity or practice that masters the divine power within.

❖ ❖ ❖

When you go beyond the consciousness of this world, knowing that you are not the body or the mind, and yet aware as never before that you exist—that divine consciousness is what you are. You are That in which is rooted everything in the universe.

❖ ❖ ❖

Shatter the frames of limitations, which separate your soul from Spirit.

"Am I the ocean? It is too small,
A dream dewdrop on the azure blades of space.
Am I the sky? It is too small,
A lake in the bosom of eternity.
Am I eternity? It is too small,
Framed in a name.
In the vast region of namelessness I love to
*   dwell,*
Beyond limits of dreams, names, conceptions.
I am what I am always—
In the ever-present past,
In the ever-present future,
In the ever-present now."

CHAPTER 15

The Consummate Goal

Mankind is engaged in an eternal quest for that "something else" he hopes will bring him happiness, complete and unending. For those individual souls who have sought and found God, the search is over: He is that Something Else.

❖ ❖ ❖

Many people may doubt that finding God is the purpose of life; but everyone can accept the idea that the purpose of life is to find happiness. I say that God is Happiness. He is Bliss. He is Love. He is Joy that will never go away from your soul. So why shouldn't you try to acquire that Happiness? No one else can give it to you. You must continuously cultivate it yourself.

❖ ❖ ❖

Even if life gave you at one time everything you wanted—wealth, power, friends—after a while you would again become dissatisfied and need something more. But there is one thing that can never become stale to you—joy itself. Happiness that is delightfully varied, though its essence is changeless, is the inner experience everyone is seeking. Lasting, ever new joy is God. Finding this Joy within, you will find it in everything without. In God you will tap the Reservoir of perennial, unending bliss.

❖ ❖ ❖

Suppose you are going to be punished by not being allowed to go to sleep when you are desperately in need of rest, and suddenly someone says: "All right, you may go to sleep now." Think of the joy you would feel just before falling asleep. Multiply that one million times! Still it would not describe the joy felt in communion with God.

❖ ❖ ❖

The joy of God is boundless, unceasing, all the time new. Body, mind, nothing can disturb you when you are in that consciousness—such is the grace and glory of the Lord. And He will explain to you whatever you haven't been able to understand; everything you want to know.

❖ ❖ ❖

When you sit in the silence of deep meditation, joy bubbles up from within, roused by no outer stimulus. The joy of meditation is overwhelming. Those who have not gone into the silence of true meditation do not know what real joy is.

❖ ❖ ❖

As the mind and the feeling are directed inward, you begin to feel God's joy. The pleasures of the senses do not last; but the joy of God is everlasting. It is incomparable!

❖ ❖ ❖

Making Time for God in Your Life

Everything has its place, but when you waste time at the cost of your true happiness it is not good. I dropped every unnecessary activity so that I could meditate and try to know God, so that I could day and night be in His divine consciousness.

❖ ❖ ❖

Very few of us know how much we can put into life if we use it properly, wisely, and economically. Let us economize our time—lifetimes ebb away before we wake up, and that is why we do not realize the value of the immortal time God has given us.

❖ ❖ ❖

Do not while away your time in idleness. A great many people occupy themselves with inconsequential activities. Ask them what they have been doing and they will usually say, "Oh, I have been busy every minute!" But they can scarcely remember what they were so busy about!

❖ ❖ ❖

In an instant you may be required to leave this world; you will have to cancel all your engagements. Why then give any other activity first importance, with the result that you have no time for God? That is not common sense. It is because of *maya*, the net of cosmic delusion which is thrown over us, that we entangle ourselves in mundane interests and forget the Lord.

❖ ❖ ❖

Belief in the necessity of fulfilling lesser desires and duties first is man's greatest delusion. I well remember that during my training as a young disciple of my guru, Swami Sri Yukteswarji, I kept promising myself daily, "I will meditate longer tomorrow." A whole year slipped by before I realized that I was still putting it off. At once I made a resolution that first thing in the morning I would clean my body and then meditate long. But even then, as soon as I stirred about I became caught up in my daily duties and activities. Thereupon I resolved to have my meditation first. Thus I learned a great lesson: First comes my duty to God, and then I take care of all lesser duties.

❖ ❖ ❖

It is important to differentiate between your needs and your wants. Your needs are few, while your wants can be limitless. In order to find freedom and Bliss, minister only to your needs. Stop creating limitless wants and pursuing the will-o'-the-wisp of false happiness.

❖ ❖ ❖

"What is the best prayer?" a disciple inquired. Paramahansa Yogananda replied:

"Say to the Lord: 'Please tell me Thy will.' Don't say: 'I want this and I want that,' but have faith that He knows what you need. You will see that you get much better things when He chooses for you."

❖ ❖ ❖

If you have no success in receiving some little toy of matter with which you are infatuated, be not resentful toward God. Sometimes it is good that we do not get the things we want. When the Divine Father sees that His impulsive children want to plunge into the flames of wrong or excessive desires, lured by their luminosity, He tries to protect them from being burned.

God says: "When My children think they do not receive from Me any response to their prayers, they know not that I do answer—only differently from what they expect of Me. I will not always respond according to their wishes, until they have attained perfection. Only when they are perfect will their requests be governed always by wisdom."

❖ ❖ ❖

It is not wrong to tell the Lord that we want something, but it shows greater faith if we simply say: "Heavenly Father, I know that Thou dost anticipate my every need. Sustain me according to Thy will."

If a man is eager to own a car, for instance, and prays for it with sufficient intensity, he will receive it. But possession of a car may not be the best thing for him. Sometimes the Lord denies our little prayers because He intends to bestow on us a better gift. Trust more in God. Believe that He who created you will maintain you.

❖ ❖ ❖

God has proven that when He is with me all the "necessities of life" become unnecessary. In that consciousness you become more healthy than the average person, more joyous, more bountiful in every way. Don't seek little things; they will divert you from God. Start your experiment now: make life simple and be a king.

❖ ❖ ❖

The ordinary person is influenced by his worldly environment. The man of concentration shapes his own life. He plans his day and finds at the end of the day that his plans are carried out; he finds himself nearer to God and his goal. A weak man plans many wonderful things, but finds at the end of the day that he has been a victim of circumstances and bad habits. Such a person usually blames everyone but himself.

Remember, you should blame no one but yourself for your troubles. If you make up your mind that you are going to control your circumstances according to law, your circumstances will adjust themselves accordingly. Eventually you must learn to lead a controlled existence.

❖ ❖ ❖

You are the master of the moments of your life.

❖ ❖ ❖

Suppose you tell yourself, "Now today I will find time to meditate." *Do* it; sit for at least a few minutes. The next day, resolve to stay a little longer in meditation. And the next day, in spite of obstacles, make a little more effort.

❖ ❖ ❖

Not until you feel in your consciousness the absolute importance of God will you reach Him. Do not permit life to cheat you. Form those good habits that make for true happiness. Follow a simple diet, exercise the body, and meditate daily—no matter what happens, rain or shine. If you are unable to exercise and meditate in the morning, do it at night. Pray to Him every day, "Lord, even if I die, or if the whole world crumbles away, I am going to find time daily to be with Thee."

❖ ❖ ❖

The minutes are more important than the years. If you do not fill the minutes of your life with thoughts of God, the years will slip by; and when you need Him most you may be unable to feel His presence. But if you fill the minutes of your life with divine aspirations, automatically the years will be saturated with them.

Practicing the Presence of God

Joy lies in continually thinking of God. The longing for Him should be constant. A time comes when your mind never wanders away, when not even the greatest affliction of body, mind, and soul can take your consciousness from the living presence of God. Is that not wonderful? to live and think and feel God all the time? to remain in the castle of His presence, whence death nor aught else can take you away?

❖ ❖ ❖

Just behind the words of your speech, just behind your thoughts, just behind the love of your heart, just behind your will, just behind your sense of I-ness, is the great spirit of God. For those who think Him far away, He is far away; but for those who think Him near, He is ever near. The Bhagavad Gita says, "He who perceives Me everywhere and beholds everything in Me never loses sight of Me, nor do I ever lose sight of him."* The Lord never fails us.

❖ ❖ ❖

We say that God is invisible to us, but in reality He is visible in the mighty manifested universe. God is everything—not just one thing.

❖ ❖ ❖

As you look upon creation, which appears so solid and real, remember always to think of it as the thought of God, frozen into physical forms. You can condition your mind to this realization in little ways each day. Whenever you see a beautiful sunset, think to yourself: "It is God's painting on the sky." As you look into the face of each person you meet, think within: "It is God who has become that form." Apply this trend of thought to all experiences: "The

---

* Bhagavad Gita VI:30.

blood in my body is God; the reason in my mind is God; the love in my heart is God; everything that exists is God."

❖ ❖ ❖

Yoga is the art of doing everything with the consciousness of God. Not only when you are meditating, but also when you are working, your thoughts should be constantly anchored in Him. If you work with the consciousness that you are doing it to please God, that activity unites you with Him. Therefore do not imagine that you can find God only in meditation. Both meditation and right activity are essential, as the Bhagavad Gita teaches. If you think of God while you perform your duties in this world, you will be mentally united with Him.

❖ ❖ ❖

When you work for God, not self, it is just as good as meditation. Then work helps your meditation and meditation helps your work. You need the balance. With meditation only, you become lazy. With activity only, the mind becomes worldly and you forget God.

❖ ❖ ❖

Doing things for God is a very personal experience, so satisfying.

❖ ❖ ❖

It is when you persistently, selflessly perform every action with love-inspired thoughts of God that He will come to you. Then you realize that you are the Ocean of Life, which has become the tiny wave of each life. This is the way of knowing the Lord through activity. When in every action you think of Him before you act, while you are performing the action, and after you have finished it, He will reveal Himself to you. You must work, but let God work through you; this is the best part of devotion. If you are constantly thinking that He is walking through your feet, working through your hands, accomplishing through your will, you will know Him.

❖ ❖ ❖

No matter what you may be doing you are always free to whisper your love to God, until you consciously receive His response. This is the surest way to contact Him in the mad rush of present-day life.

❖ ❖ ❖

Of greatest help in your development is the habit of mental whispering to God. You will see a change in yourself that you will like very much. No matter what you do, God should be constantly in your mind. When you want to see a special show, or to buy a dress or a car you have admired, is it not true that no matter what else you may be doing your mind is continually thinking how you can get those things? Until you fulfill your strong desires, your mind will not rest; it ceaselessly works toward fulfilling those desires. Your mind should be on God night and day in the same way. Transmute petty desires into one great desire for Him. Your mind should continually whisper, "Night and day, night and day, I look for Thee night and day."*

❖ ❖ ❖

That is the philosophy of life by which we should live. Not tomorrow, but today, this minute. There cannot be any excuse for not thinking of God. Day and night, rolling in the background of your mind, God! God! God! instead of money or sex or fame. Whether you are washing dishes or digging a ditch or working in an office or a garden—whatever you may be doing—inwardly say, "Lord, manifest to me! You are right here. You are in the sun. You are in the grass. You are in the water. You are in this room. You are in my heart."

❖ ❖ ❖

Every thought we think sets up a particular subtle vibration....When you mentally utter the word "God," and keep on repeating that thought within, it sets up a vibration that invokes the presence of God.

❖ ❖ ❖

Whenever your mind wanders in the maze of myriad worldly thoughts, patiently lead it back to remembrance of the indwelling Lord. In time you will find Him ever with you—a God who talks with you in your own language, a God whose face peeps at you from every flower and shrub and blade of grass. Then

---

* From "Door of My Heart," published in *Cosmic Chants* by Paramahansa Yogananda.

you shall say: "I am free! I am clothed in the gossamer of Spirit; I fly from earth to heaven on wings of light." And what joy will consume your being!

Establishing a Relationship With God

"It hardly seems practical to think about God all the time," a visitor remarked. Paramahansaji replied:

"The world agrees with you, and is the world a happy place? True joy eludes the man who forsakes God, because He is Bliss Itself. On earth His devotees live in an inner heaven of peace; but those who forget Him pass their days in a self-created hades of insecurity and disappointment. To 'make friends' with the Lord is to be really practical!"

❖ ❖ ❖

Cultivate His acquaintance. It is possible to know God just as well as you know your dearest friend. That is the truth.

❖ ❖ ❖

First you must have a right concept of God—a definite idea through which you can form a relationship with Him—and then you must meditate and pray until that mental conception becomes changed into actual perception. Then you will know Him. If you persist, the Lord will come.

❖ ❖ ❖

There are people who depict their Creator as one

who imperiously tests man with the smoke of ignorance and the fire of punishment, and who judges man's actions with heartless scrutiny. They thus distort the true concept of God as a loving, compassionate Heavenly Father into a false image of one who is a strict, unsparing, and vengeful tyrant. But devotees who commune with God know it is foolish to think of Him otherwise than as the Compassionate Being who is the infinite receptacle of all love and goodness.

❖ ❖ ❖

God is Eternal Bliss. His being is love, wisdom, and joy. He is both impersonal and personal, and manifests Himself in whatever way He pleases. He appears before His saints in the form each of them holds dear: a Christian sees Christ, a Hindu beholds Krishna or the Divine Mother, and so on. Devotees whose worship takes an impersonal turn become conscious of the Lord as an infinite Light or as the wondrous sound of *Aum*, the primal Word, the Holy Ghost. The highest experience man can have is to feel that Bliss in which every other aspect of Divinity—love, wisdom, immortality—is fully contained.

But how can I convey to you in words the nature of God? He is ineffable, indescribable. Only in deep meditation shall you know His unique essence.

Proof of God's Response

"Sir, I do not seem to be progressing in my

meditations. I see and hear nothing," a student said. Paramahansa Yogananda replied:

"Seek God for His own sake. The highest perception is to feel Him as Bliss, welling up from your infinite depths. Don't yearn for visions, spiritual phenomena, or thrilling experiences. The path to the Divine is not a circus!"

❖ ❖ ❖

A common cause of spiritual discouragement is the devotee's expectation that God's response will come in a great blaze of awe-inspiring inner illumination. This erroneous notion dulls the devotee's perception of the subtle Divine responses that are present from the very beginning of one's meditative practices. God responds to the devotee's every effort, every devotional call. Even as a novice, you will realize this in your own seeking if you learn to recognize Him as the quiet, inner peace that steals over your consciousness. This peace is the first proof of God's presence within. You will know it is He who has guided and inspired you to some right decision in your life. You will feel His strength empowering you to overcome bad habits and nurture spiritual qualities. You will know Him as the ever-increasing joy and love that surges deep within, overflowing into your everyday life and relationships.

❖ ❖ ❖

The more you feel peace in meditation, the closer you are to God. He moves nearer and nearer to you the deeper you enter into meditation. The peace of meditation is the language and embracing comfort of God. Therefore, God is present right on the throne of peace within you. Find Him there first and you will find Him in all the noble pursuits of life, in true friends, in the beauty of nature, in good books, in good thoughts, in noble aspirations....When you know God as peace within, then you will realize Him as peace existing in the universal harmony of all things without.

❖ ❖ ❖

"Though I try to calm my mind, I lack the power to banish restless thoughts and to penetrate the world within," a visitor remarked. "I must be lacking in devotion."

"Sitting in the silence trying to feel devotion may often get you nowhere," Paramahansa Yogananda said. "That is why I teach scientific techniques of meditation. Practice them and you will be able to disconnect the mind from sensory distractions and from the otherwise ceaseless flow of thoughts.

"By *Kriya Yoga* one's consciousness functions on a higher plane; devotion to the Infinite Spirit then arises spontaneously in man's heart."

❖ ❖ ❖

The essential proof of Self-realization—of God's consciousness in you—is to be truly and unconditionally happy. If you are receiving more and more joy in meditation, without cessation, you may know that God is making manifest His presence in you.

❖ ❖ ❖

Even true devotees think sometimes that God does not answer their prayers. He does answer silently, through His laws; but until He is absolutely sure of the devotee He will not answer openly, He will not talk to the devotee. The Lord of Universes is so humble that He does not speak, lest in so doing He influence the devotee's use of free will to choose or reject Him. Once you know Him, there is no doubt that you will love Him. Who could resist the Irresistible? But you have to prove your unconditional love for God in order to know Him. You have to have faith. You have to know that even as you pray He is listening to you. Then He will make Himself known to you.

❖ ❖ ❖

When God does not respond to your prayers, it is because you are not in earnest. If you offer Him dry imitation prayers, you cannot expect to claim the Heavenly Father's attention. The only way to reach God through prayer is by persistence, regularity, and depth of earnestness. Cleanse your mind of all negation, such as fear, worry, anger; then fill it with thoughts of love, service, and joyous expectation. In the sanctum of your heart there must be enshrined one power, one joy, one peace—God.

The Personal Element in the Search for God

There is a personal element in the search for God

that is more important than mastery over the whole
science of Yoga. The Heavenly Father wants to be
sure that His children desire only Him, that they
will not be satisfied with anything else. When God
is made to feel that He is not first in the devotee's
heart, He stands aside. But to him who says, "O
Lord, it matters not if I lose sleep tonight, so long as
I am with Thee," He will come. Positively! From behind the countless screens of this mysterious world
the Ruler of creation will come forth to reveal Himself behind each one. He talks to His true devotees,
and plays hide-and-seek with them. Sometimes He
suddenly unveils a comforting truth when one is
worried. In time, and in direct or indirect ways, He
grants every wish of His devotee.

❖ ❖ ❖

To coax God to give Himself takes steady, unceasing zeal. Nobody can teach you that zeal. You
have to develop that yourself. "You can take a horse
to water but you cannot make him drink." Yet when
the horse is thirsty it seeks out water with zeal. So,
when you have an immense thirst for the Divine,
when you will not give undue importance to anything else—the tests of the world or the tests of the
body—then He will come.

❖ ❖ ❖

The greatest factor for success with God is to
have that resolute desire.

❖ ❖ ❖

Though God hears all our prayers He does not always respond. Our situation is like that of a child who calls for his mother, but the mother does not think it necessary to come. She sends him a plaything to keep him quiet. But when the child refuses to be comforted by anything except the mother's presence, she comes. If you want to know God, you must be like the naughty baby who cries till the mother comes.

❖ ❖ ❖

Do not jump up after only one or two mental broadcasts, but with continuous personal zeal keep on consciously [affirming] with the ever-increasing hunger of your heart, incessantly...until you feel the ever-increasing thrill of joy bursting in your whole body.

❖ ❖ ❖

When you feel a bursting thrill of joy expanding in your heart and your whole body, and it continues to increase even after meditation, you have received the one sure proof that God has answered through the devotion-tuned radio of your heart.

❖ ❖ ❖

In Him you will find all the love of all hearts. You will find completeness. Everything that the world gives you and then takes away, leaving you in pain or disillusionment, you will find in God in a much greater way, and with no aftermath of sorrow.

❖ ❖ ❖

He is the nearest of the near, the dearest of the dear. Love Him as a miser loves money, as an ardent man loves his sweetheart, as a drowning person loves breath. When you yearn for God with intensity, He will come to you.

❖ ❖ ❖

The Searcher of Hearts wants only your sincere love. He is like a little child: someone may offer Him his whole wealth and He doesn't want it; and another cries to Him, "O Lord, I love you!" and into that devotee's heart He comes running.

❖ ❖ ❖

God will not tell you that you should desire Him above all else, because He wants your love to be freely given, without "prompting." That is the whole secret in the game of this universe. He who created us yearns for our love. He wants us to give it spontaneously, without His asking. Our love is the one thing God does not possess, unless we choose to bestow it. So, you see, even the Lord has something to attain: our love. And we shall never be happy until we give it.

❖ ❖ ❖

The greatest love you can experience is in communion with God in meditation. The love between the soul and Spirit is the perfect love, the love you are all seeking. When you meditate, love grows. Millions of thrills pass through your heart....If you meditate deeply, a love will come over you such as no human tongue can describe; you will know His divine love, and you will be able to give that pure love to others.

❖ ❖ ❖

If you could feel even a particle of divine love, so great would be your joy—so overpowering—you could not contain it.

❖ ❖ ❖

If we are attuned to God, our perception is limitless, pervading everywhere in the oceanic flow of the Divine Presence. When the Spirit is known, and when we know ourselves as Spirit, there is no land or sea, no earth or sky—all is He. The melting of everything in Spirit is a state no one can describe. A great bliss is felt—eternal fullness of joy and knowledge and love.

❖ ❖ ❖

The love of God, the love of the Spirit, is an all-consuming love. Once you have experienced it, it shall lead you on and on in the eternal realms. That love will never be taken away from your heart. It shall burn there, and in its fire you shall find the great magnetism of Spirit that draws others unto you, and attracts whatsoever you truly need or desire.

I tell you truthfully that all my questions have been answered, not through man but through God. He *is*. He *is*. It is His spirit that talks to you through me. It is His love that I speak of. Thrill after thrill! Like gentle zephyrs His love comes over the soul. Day and night, week after week, year after year, it goes on increasing—you don't know where the end is. And that is what you are seeking, every one of you. You think you want human love and prosperity, but behind these it is your Father who is calling you. If you realize He is greater than all His gifts, you will find Him.

❖ ❖ ❖

Man has come on earth solely to learn to know God; he is here for no other reason. This is the true message of the Lord. To all those who seek and love Him, He tells of that great Life where there is no pain, no old age, no war, no death—only eternal assurance. In that Life nothing is destroyed. There is only ineffable happiness that will never grow stale—a happiness always new.

So that is why it is worthwhile to seek God. All those who sincerely seek Him will surely find Him. Those who want to love the Lord and yearn to enter His kingdom, and who sincerely wish in their hearts to know Him, will find Him. You must have an ever-increasing desire for Him, day and night. He will acknowledge your love by fulfilling His promise to you throughout eternity, and you shall know joy and happiness unending. All is light, all is joy, all is peace, all is love. He is all.

❖ ❖ ❖

Prayers and Affirmations

Teach me to find Thy presence on the altar of my constant peace and in the joy that springs from deep meditation.

❖ ❖ ❖

Bless me, that I may find Thee in the temple of each thought and activity. Finding Thee within, I will find Thee without, in all people, and in all conditions.

About the Author

"The ideal of love for God and service to humanity found full expression in the life of Paramahansa Yogananda....Though the major part of his life was spent outside India, still he takes his place among our great saints. His work continues to grow and shine ever more brightly, drawing people everywhere on the path of the pilgrimage of the Spirit."

—from a tribute by the Government of India upon issuing a commemorative stamp in Paramahansa Yogananda's honor on the twenty-fifth anniversary of his passing

Born in India on January 5, 1893, Paramahansa Yogananda devoted his life to helping people of all races and creeds to realize and express more fully in their lives the beauty, nobility, and true divinity of the human spirit.

After graduating from Calcutta University in 1915, Sri Yogananda took formal vows as a monk of India's venerable monastic Swami Order. Two years later, he began his life's work with the founding of a "how-to-live" school—since grown to seventeen educational institutions throughout India—where traditional academic subjects were offered together with yoga training and instruction in spiritual ideals. In 1920, he was invited to serve as India's delegate to an International Congress of Religious Liberals in Boston. His address to the Congress and subsequent lectures on the East Coast were enthusiastically received, and in 1924 he embarked on a cross-continental speaking tour.

Over the next three decades, Paramahansa Yogananda contributed in far-reaching ways to a greater awareness and appreciation in the West of the spiritual wisdom of the East. In Los Angeles, he established an international headquarters for Self-Realization Fellowship—the nonsectarian religious society he had founded in 1920. Through his writings, extensive lecture tours, and the creation of numerous Self-Realization Fellowship temples and meditation centers, he introduced thousands of truth-seekers to the ancient science and philosophy of Yoga and its universally applicable methods of meditation.

Today, the spiritual and humanitarian work begun by Paramahansa Yogananda continues under the direction of Brother Chidananda, president of Self-Realization Fellowship/Yogoda Satsanga Society of India. In addition to publishing his lectures, writings, and informal talks (including a comprehensive series of lessons for home study), the society also oversees its temples, retreats, and centers around the world; the monastic communities of the Self-Realization Order; and a Worldwide Prayer Circle.

In an article on Sri Yogananda's life and work, Dr. Quincy Howe, Jr., Professor of Ancient Languages at Scripps College, wrote: "Paramahansa Yogananda brought to the West not only India's perennial promise of God-realization, but also a practical method by which spiritual aspirants from all walks of life may progress rapidly toward that goal. Originally appreciated in the West only on the most lofty and abstract level, the spiritual legacy of India is now accessible as practice and experience to all who aspire to know God, not in the beyond, but in the here and now....Yogananda has placed within the reach of all the most exalted methods of contemplation."

The life and teachings of Paramahansa Yogananda are described in his *Autobiography of a Yogi* (see page 221). An award-winning documentary film about his life and work, *Awake: The Life of Yogananda,* was released in October 2014.

PARAMAHANSA YOGANANDA:
A Yogi in Life and Death

Paramahansa Yogananda entered *mahasamadhi* (a yogi's final conscious exit from the body) in Los Angeles, California, on March 7, 1952, after concluding his speech at a banquet held in honor of H. E. Binay R. Sen, Ambassador of India.

The great world teacher demonstrated the value of yoga (scientific techniques for God-realization) not only in life but in death. Weeks after his departure his unchanged face shone with the divine luster of incorruptibility.

Mr. Harry T. Rowe, Los Angeles Mortuary Director, Forest Lawn Memorial-Park (in which the body of the great master is temporarily placed), sent Self-Realization Fellowship a notarized letter from which the following extracts are taken:

"The absence of any visual signs of decay in the dead body of Paramahansa Yogananda offers the most extraordinary case in our experience....No physical disintegration was visible in his body even twenty days after death....No indication of mold was visible on his skin, and no visible desiccation (drying up) took place in the bodily tissues. This state of perfect preservation of a body is, so far as we know from mortuary annals, an unparalleled one....At the time of receiving Yogananda's body, the Mortuary personnel expected to observe, through the glass lid of the casket, the usual progressive signs of bodily decay. Our astonishment increased as day followed day without bringing any visible change in the body under observation. Yogananda's body was apparently in a phenomenal state of immutability....

"No odor of decay emanated from his body at any time....The physical appearance of Yogananda on March 27th, just before the bronze cover of the casket was put into position, was the same as it had been on March 7th. He looked on March 27th as fresh and as unravaged by decay as he had looked on the night of his death. On March 27th there was no reason to say that his body had suffered any visible physical disintegration at all. For these reasons we state again that the case of Paramahansa Yogananda is unique in our experience."

Additional Resources on the Kriya Yoga Teachings of Paramahansa Yogananda

Self-Realization Fellowship is dedicated to freely assisting seekers worldwide. For information regarding our annual series of public lectures and classes, meditation and inspirational services at our temples and centers around the world, a schedule of retreats, and other activities, we invite you to visit our website or our International Headquarters:

www.yogananda-srf.org

Self-Realization Fellowship
3880 San Rafael Avenue
Los Angeles, CA 90065
(323) 225-2471

SELF-REALIZATION FELLOWSHIP LESSONS

*Personal guidance and instruction from
Paramahansa Yogananda on the techniques of yoga
meditation and principles of spiritual living*

If you feel drawn to the spiritual teachings of Paramahansa Yogananda, we invite you to enroll in the *Self-Realization Fellowship Lessons*.

Paramahansa Yogananda originated this home-study series to provide sincere seekers the opportunity to learn and practice the ancient yoga meditation techniques that he brought to the West—including the science of *Kriya Yoga*. The *Lessons* also present his practical guidance for attaining balanced physical, mental, and spiritual well-being.

The *Self-Realization Fellowship Lessons* are available at a nominal fee (to cover printing and postage costs). All students are freely given personal guidance in their practice by Self-Realization Fellowship monks and nuns.

For more information...

Complete details about the *Self-Realization Fellowship Lessons* are included in the free booklet *Undreamed-of Possibilities*. To receive a copy of this booklet and an application form, please visit our website or contact our International Headquarters.

AIMS AND IDEALS
of
Self-Realization Fellowship

As set forth by Paramahansa Yogananda, Founder
Brother Chidananda, President

To disseminate among the nations a knowledge of definite scientific techniques for attaining direct personal experience of God.

To teach that the purpose of life is the evolution, through self-effort, of man's limited mortal consciousness into God Consciousness; and to this end to establish Self-Realization Fellowship temples for God-communion throughout the world, and to encourage the establishment of individual temples of God in the homes and in the hearts of men.

To reveal the complete harmony and basic oneness of original Christianity as taught by Jesus Christ and original Yoga as taught by Bhagavan Krishna; and to show that these principles of truth are the common scientific foundation of all true religions.

To point out the one divine highway to which all paths of true religious beliefs eventually lead; the highway of daily, scientific, devotional meditation on God.

To liberate man from his threefold suffering: physical disease, mental inharmonies, and spiritual ignorance.

To encourage "plain living and high thinking"; and to spread a spirit of brotherhood among all peoples by teaching the eternal basis of their unity: kinship with God.

To demonstrate the superiority of mind over body, of soul over mind.

To overcome evil by good, sorrow by joy, cruelty by kindness, ignorance by wisdom.

To unite science and religion through realization of the unity of their underlying principles.

To advocate cultural and spiritual understanding between East and West, and the exchange of their finest distinctive features.

To serve mankind as one's larger Self.

Also published by Self-Realization Fellowship...

AUTOBIOGRAPHY OF A YOGI

This acclaimed autobiography presents a fascinating portrait of one of the great spiritual figures of our time. With engaging candor, eloquence, and wit, Paramahansa Yogananda narrates the inspiring chronicle of his life—the experiences of his remarkable childhood, encounters with many saints and sages during his youthful search throughout India for an illumined teacher, ten years of training in the hermitage of a revered yoga master, and the thirty years that he lived and taught in America. Also recorded here are his meetings with Mahatma Gandhi, Rabindranath Tagore, Luther Burbank, the Catholic stigmatist Therese Neumann, and other celebrated spiritual personalities of East and West.

Autobiography of a Yogi is at once a beautifully written account of an exceptional life and a profound introduction to the ancient science of Yoga and its time-honored tradition of meditation. The author clearly explains the subtle but definite laws behind both the ordinary events of everyday life and the extraordinary events commonly termed miracles. His absorbing life story thus becomes the background for a penetrating and unforgettable look at the ultimate mysteries of human existence.

Considered a modern spiritual classic, the book has been translated into forty languages and is widely used as a text and reference work in colleges and universities. A perennial best seller since it was first published more than sixty years ago, *Autobiography of a Yogi* has found its way into the hearts of millions of readers around the world.

"A rare account."—THE NEW YORK TIMES

"A fascinating and clearly annotated study."—NEWSWEEK

"There has been nothing before, written in English or in any other European language, like this presentation of Yoga."
> —COLUMBIA UNIVERSITY PRESS

Also by Paramahansa Yogananda

Available at bookstores or online at www.srfbooks.org

Autobiography of a Yogi

Autobiography of a Yogi
(Audiobook, read by Sir Ben Kingsley)

God Talks With Arjuna: The Bhagavad Gita—
A New Translation and Commentary

The Second Coming of Christ:
The Resurrection of the Christ Within You—
A Revelatory Commentary
on the Original Teachings of Jesus

The Yoga of Jesus

The Yoga of the Bhagavad Gita

The Collected Talks and Essays
Volume I: Man's Eternal Quest
Volume II: The Divine Romance
Volume III: Journey to Self-realization

Wine of the Mystic: The Rubaiyat of Omar Khayyam—
A Spiritual Interpretation

The Science of Religion

Whispers from Eternity

Songs of the Soul

Sayings of Paramahansa Yogananda

Scientific Healing Affirmations

In the Sanctuary of the Soul: A Guide to Effective Prayer

Inner Peace:
How to Be Calmly Active and Actively Calm

How You Can Talk With God

Metaphysical Meditations

The Law of Success

Cosmic Chants

A complete catalog of books and audio/video recordings including rare archival recordings of Paramahansa Yogananda is available on request.

DVD Video
Awake: The Life of Yogananda
A film by CounterPoint Films

Free Introductory Booklet: *Undreamed-of Possibilities*

The scientific techniques of meditation taught by Paramahansa Yogananda, including *Kriya Yoga,* are presented in the *Self-Realization Fellowship Lessons.* A free introductory booklet, *Undreamed-of Possibilities,* is available on our website www.yogananda-srf.org.

SELF-REALIZATION FELLOWSHIP
3880 San Rafael Avenue • Los Angeles, CA 90065-3219
tel (323) 225-2471 • fax (323) 225-5088
www.yogananda-srf.org

Glossary

astral world. Behind the physical world of matter, there exists a subtle astral world of light and energy, and a causal or ideational world of thought. Every being, every object, every vibration on the physical plane has an astral counterpart, for in the astral universe (heaven) is the "blueprint" of the material universe. At death each individual, though freed from his physical encasement, remains clothed in an astral body of light (similar in appearance to the earthly form left behind) and a causal body of thought. He ascends to one of the many vibratory regions of the astral world ("In my Father's house are many mansions." — John 14:2) to continue his spiritual evolution in the greater freedom of that subtle realm. There he remains for a karmically predetermined time until physical rebirth. (See *reincarnation*.)

Aum (Om). The Sanskrit root word or seed-sound symbolizing that aspect of Godhead which creates and sustains all things; Cosmic Vibration. *Aum* of the Vedas became the sacred word *Hum* of the Tibetans; *Amin* of the Moslems; and *Amen* of the Egyptians, Greeks, Romans, Jews, and Christians. The world's great religions state that all created things originate in the cosmic vibratory energy of *Aum* or Amen, the Word or Holy Ghost. "In the beginning was the Word, and the Word was with God, and the Word was God.... All things were made by him [the Word or *Aum*]; and without him was not any thing made that was made" (John 1:1,3).

Amen in Hebrew means *sure, faithful.* "These things saith the Amen, the faithful and true witness, the beginning of the creation of God" (Revelation 3:14).

Even as sound is produced by the vibration of a running motor, so the omnipresent sound of Aum faithfully testifies to the running of the "Cosmic Motor," which upholds all life and every particle of creation through vibratory energy. In the *Self-Realization Fellowship Lessons* (*q.v.*), Paramahansa Yogananda teaches techniques of meditation whose practice brings direct experience of God as *Aum* or Holy Ghost. That blissful communion with the invisible divine Power ("the Comforter, which is the Holy Ghost"—John 14:26) is the truly scientific basis of prayer.

avatar. Divine incarnation; from the Sanskrit *avatara*, with roots *ava*, "down," and *tri*, "to pass." One who attains union with Spirit and then returns to earth to help mankind is called an avatar.

Bhagavad Gita. "Song of the Lord." An ancient Indian scripture consisting of eighteen chapters from the *Mahabharata* epic. Presented in the form of a dialogue between the avatar (*q.v.*) Lord Krishna and his disciple Arjuna on the eve of the historic battle of Kurukshetra, the Gita is a profound treatise on the science of Yoga (union with God) and a timeless prescription for happiness and success in everyday living. Of this universal scripture Mahatma Gandhi wrote: "Those who will meditate on the Gita will derive fresh joy and new meanings from it every day. There is not a single spiritual tangle which the Gita cannot unravel."

The quotations from the Bhagavad Gita in the text and footnotes of this book are from translations by Paramahansa Yogananda, which he rendered from the Sanskrit sometimes literally and sometimes in paraphrase.

Bhagavan Krishna. An avatar (*q.v.*) who lived in ancient India ages before the Christian era. One of the

meanings given for the word *Krishna* in the Hindu
scriptures is "Omniscient Spirit." Thus, *Krishna*, like
Christ, is a title signifying the spiritual magnitude of
the avatar—his oneness with God. (See *Christ Consciousness*.) The title *Bhagavan* means "Lord."

chakras. In Yoga, the seven occult centers of life and consciousness in the spine and brain, which enliven the
physical and astral bodies of man. These centers are
referred to as *chakras* ("wheels") because the concentrated energy in each one is like a hub from which
radiate rays of lifegiving light and energy. In ascending
order, these *chakras* are *muladhara* (the coccygeal, at
the base of the spine); *svadhisthana* (the sacral, two
inches above *muladhara*); *manipura* (the lumbar, opposite the navel); *anahata* (the dorsal, opposite the heart);
vishuddha (the cervical, at the base of the neck); *ajna*
(traditionally located between the eyebrows; in actu-
ality, directly connected by polarity with the medulla;
see also *medulla* and *spiritual eye*); and *sahasrara* (in
the uppermost part of the cerebrum).

The seven centers are divinely planned exits or
"trap doors" through which the soul has descended
into the body and through which it must reascend by
a process of meditation. By seven successive steps, the
soul escapes into Cosmic Consciousness. In its conscious upward passage through the seven opened or
"awakened" cerebrospinal centers, the soul travels the
highway to the Infinite, the true path by which the
soul must retrace its course to reunite with God.

Yoga treatises generally consider only the six lower
centers as *chakras*, with *sahasrara* referred to sepa-
rately as a seventh center. All seven centers, however,
are often referred to as lotuses, whose petals open, or

turn upward, in spiritual awakening as the life and consciousness travel up the spine

Christ center. The center of concentration and will in the body, at the point between the eyebrows. Seat of Christ Consciousness (*q.v.*) and of the spiritual eye (*q.v.*).

Christ Consciousness. "Christ" or "Christ Consciousness" is the projected consciousness of God immanent in all creation. In Christian scripture it is called the "only begotten son," the only pure reflection in creation of God the Father; in Hindu scripture it is called *Kutastha Chaitanya,* the cosmic intelligence of Spirit everywhere present in creation. It is the universal consciousness, oneness with God, manifested by Jesus, Krishna, and other avatars. Great saints and yogis know it as the state of samadhi (*q.v.*) meditation wherein their consciousness has become identified with the intelligence in every particle of creation; they feel the entire universe as their own body.

Cosmic Consciousness. The Absolute; Spirit beyond creation. Also the *samadhi*-meditation state of oneness with God both beyond and within vibratory creation.

Divine Mother. The aspect of God that is active in creation; the *shakti,* or power, of the Transcendent Creator. Other terms for this aspect of Divinity are Nature or *Prakriti, Aum,* Holy Ghost, Cosmic Intelligent Vibration. Also, the personal aspect of God as Mother, embodying the Lord's love and compassionate qualities.

The Hindu scriptures teach that God is both immanent and transcendent, personal and impersonal. He may be sought as the Absolute; as one of His manifest eternal qualities, such as love, wisdom, bliss, light; or in a concept such as Heavenly Father, Mother, Friend.

egoism. The ego-principle, *ahamkara* in Sanskrit (lit., "I do"), is the root cause of dualism or the seeming separation between man and his Creator. Egoism brings human beings under the sway of *maya* (*q.v.*), by which the soul becomes delusively identified with the limitations of body-consciousness and forgets its oneness with God, the Sole Doer. (See *Self.*)

guru. Spiritual teacher. Though the word *guru* is often misused to refer simply to any teacher or instructor, a true God-illumined guru is one who, in his attainment of self-mastery, has realized his identity with the omnipresent Spirit. Such a one is uniquely qualified to lead the seeker on his or her inward journey toward divine realization.

karma. Effects of past actions, from this or previous lifetimes; from the Sanskrit *kri*, to do. The equilibrating law of karma is that of action and reaction, cause and effect, sowing and reaping. In the course of natural righteousness, every human being by his thoughts and actions becomes the molder of his own destiny. Whatever energies he himself, wisely or unwisely, has set in motion must return to him as their starting point, like a circle inexorably completing itself. An understanding of karma as the law of justice serves to free the human mind from resentment against God and man. A person's karma follows him from incarnation to incarnation until fulfilled or spiritually transcended. (See *reincarnation.*)

Krishna. See *Bhagavan Krishna.*

Kriya Yoga. A sacred spiritual science, originating millenniums ago in India. It includes certain techniques of meditation (*q.v.*) whose devoted practice leads to direct, personal experience of God. *Kriya*, a form of *Raja* ("royal" or "complete") *Yoga,* is extolled by Krishna in the Bhagavad Gita and by Patanjali in the *Yoga Sutras. Kriya Yoga* was revived in this age by Mahavatar Babaji *(q.v.),* who chose Paramahansa Yogananda to make this holy science available worldwide and to establish a society to insure that it would be preserved in pure form for future generations. *Kriya Yoga* is explained in chapter 26 of *Autobiography of a Yogi,* and is taught to students of the *Self-Realization Fellowship Lessons* who fulfill certain spiritual requirements.

Lahiri Mahasaya. Lahiri was the family name of Shyama Charan Lahiri (1828–1895). *Mahasaya,* a Sanskrit religious title, means "large-minded." Lahiri Mahasaya was a disciple of Mahavatar Babaji, and the guru of Swami Sri Yukteswar (Paramahansa Yogananda's guru). Lahiri Mahasaya was the one to whom Babaji revealed the ancient, almost lost science of Kriya Yoga *(q.v.).* A seminal figure in the renaissance of Yoga in modern India, he gave instruction and blessing to countless seekers who came to him, without regard to caste or creed. He was a Christlike teacher with miraculous powers; but also a family man with business responsibilities, who demonstrated for the modern world how an ideally balanced life can be achieved by combining meditation with right performance of outer duties. Lahiri Mahasaya's life is described in *Autobiography of a Yogi.*

Mahavatar Babaji. The deathless *mahavatar* ("great avatar") who in 1861 taught *Kriya Yoga (q.v.)* to Lahiri Mahasaya, and thereby restored to the world the spiritual science that had been lost for centuries. More information about his life and spiritual mission is given in *Autobiography of a Yogi.* (See *avatar.)*

maya. The delusory power inherent in the structure of

creation, by which the One appears as many. *Maya* is the principle of relativity, inversion, contrast, duality, oppositional states; the "Satan" (lit., in Hebrew, "the adversary") of the Old Testament prophets; and the "devil" whom Christ described picturesquely as a "murderer" and a "liar," because "there is no truth in him" (John 8:44).

Paramahansa Yogananda wrote:

"The Sanskrit word *maya* means 'the measurer'; it is the magical power in creation by which limitations and divisions are apparently present in the Immeasurable and Inseparable. *Maya* is Nature herself — the phenomenal worlds, ever in transitional flux as antithesis to Divine Immutability.

"In God's plan and play (*lila*), the sole function of Satan or *maya* is to attempt to divert man from Spirit to matter, from Reality to unreality. 'The devil sinneth from the beginning. For this purpose the Son of God was manifested, that he might destroy the works of the devil' (I John 3:8). That is, the manifestation of Christ Consciousness, within man's own being, effortlessly destroys the illusions or 'works of the devil.'

"*Maya* is the veil of transitoriness in Nature, the ceaseless becoming of creation; the veil that each man must lift in order to see behind it the Creator, the changeless Immutable, eternal Reality.

"Man is able to create both matter and consciousness in an illusory dream world; therefore it should not be difficult for him to realize that Spirit, utilizing the power of *maya*, has created for man a dream world of 'life' or conscious existence that in essence is as false (because ephemeral, ever changing) as are man's experiences in the dream state....Man in his mortal aspect dreams of dualities and contrasts — life and death, health and disease, happiness and sorrow; but when he awakens in soul consciousness all dualities disappear and he knows himself as the eternal and blissful Spirit."

meditation. Concentration upon God. The term is used in a general sense to denote practice of any technique for interiorizing the attention and focusing it on some aspect of God. In the specific sense, meditation refers to the end result of successful practice of such techniques: direct experience of God through intuitive perception. It is the seventh step (*dhyana*) of the eightfold path of Yoga described by Patanjali, achieved only after one has attained that fixed concentration within whereby he is completely undisturbed by sensory impressions from the outer world. In deepest meditation one experiences the eighth step of the Yoga path: *samadhi* (*q.v.*), communion, oneness with God. (See also *Yoga*.)

medulla. The principal point of entry of life force (*prana*) into the body; seat of the sixth cerebrospinal center, whose function is to receive and direct the incoming flow of cosmic energy. The life force is stored in the seventh center (*sahasrara*) in the topmost part of the brain. From that reservoir it is distributed throughout the body. The subtle center at the medulla is the main switch that controls the entrance, storage, and distribution of the life force.

paramahansa. A spiritual title signifying one who has attained the highest state of unbroken communion with God. It may be conferred only by a true guru on a qualified disciple. Swami Sri Yukteswar bestowed the title on his beloved disciple Yogananda in 1935. *Paramahansa* literally means "supreme swan." In the Hindu scriptures, the *hansa* or swan symbolizes spiritual discrimination.

prana. Life energy or life force. Intelligent, finer-than-atomic energy; life-principle of the physical cosmos and basic substance of the astral world *(q.v.)*. In the physical world, there are two kinds of *prana:* (1) the cosmic vibratory energy that is omnipresent in the universe, structuring and sustaining all things; (2) the specific *prana* or energy that pervades and sustains each human body.

Raja Yoga. The "royal" or highest path to God-union. It teaches scientific meditation *(q.v.)* as the ultimate means for realizing God, and includes the highest essentials from all other forms of Yoga. The Self-Realization Fellowship *Raja Yoga* teachings outline a way of life leading to perfect unfoldment in body, mind, and soul, based on the foundation of *Kriya Yoga (q.v.)* meditation. See *Yoga.*

reincarnation. The doctrine that human beings, compelled by the law of evolution, incarnate repeatedly in progressively higher lives—retarded by wrong actions and desires, and advanced by spiritual endeavors—until Self-realization and God-union are attained. Having thus transcended the limitations and imperfections of mortal consciousness, the soul is forever freed from compulsory reincarnation. "Him that overcometh will I make a pillar in the temple of my God, and he shall go no more out" (Revelation 3:12).

The concept of reincarnation is not exclusive to eastern philosophy, but was held as a fundamental truth of life by many ancient civilizations. The early Christian Church accepted the principle of reincarnation, which was expounded by the Gnostics and by numerous Church fathers, including Clement of Alexandria, Origen, and St. Jerome. It was not until the Second Council of Constantinople in a.d. 553 that the doctrine was officially removed from church teachings. Today many Western thinkers are beginning to adopt the concept of the law of karma (*q.v.*) and reincarnation, seeing in it a grand and reassuring explanation of life's seeming inequities.

samadhi. Ecstasy; superconscious experience; ultimately, union with God as the all-pervading supreme Reality. (See *superconsciousness* and *Yoga*.)

Self. Capitalized to denote the *atman* or soul, the divine essence of man, as distinguished from the ordinary self, which is the human personality or ego. The Self is individualized Spirit, whose essential nature is ever-existing, ever-conscious, ever-new Bliss. The Self or soul is man's inner fountainhead of love, wisdom, peace, courage, compassion, and all other divine qualities.

Self-realization. Paramahansa Yogananda has defined Self-realization as follows: "Self-realization is the knowing—in body, mind, and soul—that we are one with the omnipresence of God; that we do not have to pray that it come to us, that we are not merely near it at all times, but that God's omnipresence is our omnipresence; that we are just as much a part of Him now as we ever will be. All we have to do is improve our knowing."

Self-Realization Fellowship. The society founded by Paramahansa Yogananda in the United States in 1920 (and as Yogoda Satsanga Society of India in 1917) for disseminating worldwide the spiritual principles and meditation techniques of *Kriya Yoga* (*q.v.*). (See "About the Author," page 215.) Paramahansa Yogananda has explained that the name Self-Realization Fellowship signifies "fellowship with God through

Self-realization, and friendship with all truth-seeking souls." (See also "Aims and Ideals of Self-Realization Fellowship," page 220.)

Self-Realization Fellowship Lessons. The teachings of Paramahansa Yogananda, compiled into a comprehensive series of lessons for home study and made available to sincere truth seekers all over the world. These lessons contain the yoga meditation techniques taught by Paramahansa Yogananda, including, for those who fulfill certain requirements, *Kriya Yoga* (*q.v.*). Information about the *Lessons* is available on request from Self-Realization Fellowship International Headquarters.

spiritual eye. The single eye of intuition and omnipresent perception at the Christ (*Kutastha*) center (*q.v.*) (*ajna chakra*) between the eyebrows; the entryway into the ultimate states of divine consciousness. Jesus referred to the divine light that is perceived through the spiritual eye when he said: "When thine eye is single, thy whole body also is full of light....Take heed therefore that the light which is in thee be not darkness" (Luke 11:34–35).

Sri Yukteswar, Swami. (1855–1936). A Christlike master of modern India; guru of Paramahansa Yogananda; and author of *The Holy Science,* a treatise on the underlying unity of Christian and Hindu scriptures. Sri Yukteswarji's life is described in Paramahansa Yogananda's *Autobiography of a Yogi.*

superconsciousness. The pure, intuitive, all-seeing, ever-blissful consciousness of the soul. Sometimes used generally to refer to all the various states of God-communion experienced in meditation, but specifically the initial state, wherein one transcends ego-consciousness and realizes his Self as soul, made in the image of God. Thence follow the higher states of realization: Christ-consciousness and cosmic consciousness (*q.v.*).

Yoga. From Sanskrit *yuj,* "union." Yoga means union of the individual soul with Spirit; also, the methods by which this goal is attained. There are various types of yoga methods; the one taught by Self-Realization Fellowship is *Raja Yoga,* the "royal" or "complete" yoga taught by Bhagavan Krishna in the Bhagavad Gita. The sage Patanjali, foremost ancient exponent of Yoga, has outlined eight definite steps by which the *Raja Yogi* attains *samadhi,* or union with God. These are (1) *yama,* moral conduct; (2) *niyama,* religious observances; (3) *asana,* right posture to still bodily restlessness; (4) *pranayama,* control of *prana,* subtle life currents; (5) *pratyahara,* interiorization; (6) *dharana,* concentration; (7) *dhyana,* meditation; and (8) *samadhi,* superconscious experience.

yogi. One who practices Yoga (*q.v.*). He or she may be either married or unmarried, either a person of worldly responsibilities or one who has taken formal religious vows.

Yogoda Satsanga Society of India. The name by which Paramahansa Yogananda's society is known in India. The Society was founded by him in 1917. Its headquarters, Yogoda Math, is situated on the banks of the Ganges at Dakshineswar, near Kolkata, with a branch *math* at Ranchi, Jharkhand. In addition to meditation centers and groups throughout India, Yogoda Satsanga Society has seventeen educational institutions, from primary through college level. *Yogoda,* a word coined by Paramahansa Yogananda, is derived from *yoga,* "union, harmony, equilibrium"; and *da,* "that which imparts."

Satsanga means "divine fellowship," or "fellowship with Truth." For the West, Paramahansaji translated the Indian name as "Self-Realization Fellowship" (*q.v.*).

Index

affirmation, uses of, to awaken
true Self, 178–191; to overcome difficulties, 11, 17,
20, 33, 38 ff., 46, 67, 75,
85–86, 92, 117, 117–119,
124–125, 143, 209. *See
also* prayer

anger, overcoming, 61–62, 89,
118, 125, 136, 141 ff., 149,
157, 207

astral world, 168 ff., 224, 232

attitude, right mental, 16, 31,
37, 47, 72, 79, 80, 120, 122,
123, 124. *See also* positive
thinking

Aum, 40, 186, 204

balance, between material and
spiritual goals, 79, 94–95,
194 ff., 200; between reason and feeling, 61, 153,
154

breathing exercise, 23

Bhagavan Krishna, 35, 148,
152 n., 204, 225–26

bliss, *see* joy

calmness, 24, 34, 35, 59, 64, 74,
87 ff., 94–95, 97, 99, 125,
131, 136, 137, 138, 143,
145, 206; key to divine
perception, 5; key to solving problems, 65; nature of
God, 87

Christ center, 33, 117, 176. *See
also* spiritual eye

Christ Consciousness, 126,
148, 227, 200, 204

compassion (sympathy), 32,
53, 136, 138, 147, 148, 152,
161, 204, 227

concentration, 21, 59, 74, 81,
92, 124–25, 131, 197, 227,
230, 235; in creating and
destroying habits, 116–17;
key to finding God within,
4; key to success, 73; science of, 59, 73

conscience, inner guidance
from, 63–64, 106. *See also*
intuition

creativity, 58, 69, 75 ff., 81, 127

death, 11, 18, 19, 35, 47, 48, 56,
166 ff., 212, 195

desire for God, 194, 198, 201,
202, 207–208, 210, 212

desires, right attitude toward,
39, 59, 105, 107, 109, 110,
144, 150, 195, 196, 201–02,
207–08

devotion, key to finding God,
200–01, 202, 205 ff.

disease, *see* healing

discrimination, soul-quality of,
15, 60 ff., 76, 103, 104–05,
119. *See also* wisdom.

Divine Mother, 15, 177, 112–13,
204, 227

dream-nature of world, 30–32,
55, 79–80, 111–12, 168–69,

170; transcended through meditation, 35, 55. *See also maya*

ego, soul in delusion, 5, 31, 39, 65, 110, 114, 160

Einstein, Albert, 101n.

emotions, overcoming negative, 124 ff., 141 ff.

environment, influence of, 17, 57, 75, 103, 107, 108, 114, 130, 197

enthusiasm, 80 ff.

evenmindedness, 34–35, 46, 125, 206

evil, nature of, 15, 31, 104, 106, 110, 111, 112, 124

failure, overcoming, 16, 58, 68, 70 ff., 92, 102, 104, 126–27

faith in God, 11, 31, 38, 40, 43, 44 ff., 65, 67, 83–85, 92, 111n., 126–27, 195, 196, 207; developing, 43; different from belief, 44

fear, overcoming, 11, 31–32, 37, 46, 48, 54, 84, 89, 91 ff., 93, 142, 167, 207

forgiveness, 112, 130–131, 136, 142, 146 ff.

Francis, Saint, 12, 47

free will, 16, 207

friendship, 83, 107, 116, 135, 136, 141, 155, 160 ff., 172, 176–77, 205–206

Galli-Curci, Amelita, 158–59

getting along with others, 135 ff., 150 ff.

God, finding, *see* meditation; nature of, 4, 7, 9, 15, 38, 52, 133, 153, 192, 199–200, 203–204, 224; proof of, 39, 203–04, 205 ff., 209

guidance, receiving from within, *see* intuition

guilt, *see* sin

guru, 26

Gyanamata, Sri, 47, 175

habits, creating and destroying, 41–42, 60, 101 ff., 107, 110–11, 114 ff., 124–25, 133, 198, 205; influence on man's actions, 6–7, 42, 57, 69, 100

happiness, finding, 13, 14, 54, 78–79, 88, 89, 95–96, 102 ff., 109, 120 ff., 135, 154, 192, 193, 195, 198, 203, 206, 210, 212

hatred, overcoming, 51, 52, 84, 88, 89, 141, 142, 144, 145, 148

healing, principles of, 11, 14, 16, 18, 31, 36 ff., 40, 43, 45, 46, 48–49, 56, 58, 68, 121, 126, 197

heaven, *see* astral world

image of God, human beings made in, 3, 4, 8, 11, 14, 18, 20, 67, 79, 119, 125, 128, 133, 141–42, 152

inferiority complex, overcoming, 140, 142. *See also* soul
initiative, soul-quality of, 3, 64, 71, 75–76, 121
introspection (self-analysis), 4, 58, 61–62, 89–90, 102 ff., 121, 124, 125, 126, 140
intuition, 29, 39, 44–45, 57, 60, 63, 64 ff., 71, 75, 76, 141, 205, 231, 234–35. *See also* conscience

jealousy, overcoming, 142, 145–46
Jeans, Sir James, 101n.
Jesus Christ, 67, 84–85, 136–137, 146, 147, 154, 204, 227, 230, 232
joy, 35, 38, 42, 48, 52, 128, 130, 160, 193, 194, 197, 198, 203, 206, 207, 209, 211, 213; absence of leads to evil actions, 109; brings healing energy, 37–38; found in meditation and God-communion, 9, 48, 56, 98–99, 130, 131, 133; found through self-control, 110; nature of God, 4, 203, 204, 205, 231–232; nature of soul, 19, 114, 120, 122, 125; proof of God's presence, 39, 209

karma (law of cause and effect), overcoming, 18, 19, 20, 107, 111, 169; mass karma,

19–20, 50; soul free from karma, 18–19, 19–20
Krishna, *see* Bhagavan Krishna
Kriya Yoga, 19–20, 206, 228–29, 233–34. *See also* yoga.

Lahiri Mahasaya, 45, 64, 229
life-energy (*prana*), 8, 37–38, 80, 90–91, 98–99, 183, 232
love, 83–84, 126, 141, 142, 145, 147–48, 150 ff., 184–85, 199–200, 205, 210 ff.; answer to world's problems, 51, 52; definition of, 150; for God, 207, 210; God's, for His human children, 14, 58, 113, 211–12; human vs. divine, 150; immortality of, 172, 176; in relationships with others, 130–31, 138, 141, 142, 145, 146, 149, 150, 151, 153, 154, 155, 156, 158, 159, 160, 164, 165; nature of God, 38, 52, 189–190, 204; relation to sex, 158

maya (cosmic delusion), 9, 30, 55, 91, 106, 141, 229–30
marriage, keys to successful, 155 ff.
meditation, way to know God and the divine qualities of the soul, 5, 6, 9, 14, 18, 19, 19–20, 35, 38, 43, 54, 55, 56, 60, 63, 64, 65, 74, 76, 82, 84–85, 88, 97–98,

98–99, 109, 115–16, 117, 130, 131, 160, 186, 194, 195, 198 ff., 204 ff., 209, 210–11, 224, 225, 227, 231, 235; guided exercises, 27–29; key to world peace, 51, 52; learn to meditate, 21–29; posture for, 22, 23, 190; removes bad habits, 115–16, 118. *See also* yoga

mind, power of, 7, 13, 18–19, 33, 35, 37, 38, 41, 50, 53–54, 68, 69–70, 73, 76, 77, 88, 90, 92, 100, 101, 103, 107, 108, 114, 120, 121–22, 123, 124, 125, 141, 142, 144, 145, 171, 202–03, 228

moods, overcoming negative, 61, 88, 121, 125 ff.

money, *see* prosperity

morality, laws of, 15–16, 60, 63–64, 106, 126, 223

nervousness, overcoming, 6, 58, 88 ff., 98–99

pain, overcoming, 15, 18 ff., 34, 48, 103–04, 209, 212; banished at time of death, 169, 170, 173, 174; purpose of, 47

peace (inner), 24, 27–29, 35, 42, 78–79, 80, 84, 87, 88, 90 ff., 97–98, 99, 105, 122, 125, 130, 131, 137–38, 141–42, 143, 148, 154, 166, 174–75, 203, 205–06, 212; comes from following conscience, 63–64; condition of happiness, 88; found in simplicity, 94; found through meditation, 6, 56, 88, 94, healing power of, 87; proof of God's response, 205, 206

peace (world), 50, 51, 53

personality, 138, 154, 164; determined by one's thoughts, 100; developing attractive, 4, 138, 139, 140, 141, 150; source of, 4

positive thinking, 11, 120, 121, 123 ff., 186. *See also* attitude

power, divine, inherent in man's soul, 3, 6, 7, 11, 14, 20, 41, 67, 70, 71–72, 74, 75, 81, 140

practicing the presence of God, 198 ff.

prayer, principles of effective, 19, 26, 39, 40, 42 ff., 65, 124–25, 126, 196, 198, 207, 208, 209. *See also* affirmation

problems, 13; cause of, 16; right attitude toward, 14, 72; suggestions for solving, 11, 57 ff., 74, 81, 89–90, 118, 126

prosperity, 16, 34, 78, 79, 83 ff., 212–13

purity of heart and mind, 18–19, 61, 81, 84, 109, 114, 141, 155, 160

Raja Yoga, 26

reincarnation, 16, 100, 167, 232

relaxation, mental, 93; techniques of, 23–24, 90–91, 93

religion, meaning of, 53, 65–66, 151

Sabbath, 95, 95n.

security, finding, 36, 46, 48, 50 ff., 91, 92, 94, 143, 184–85, 203

Self, man's true nature, *see* soul

self-analysis, *see* introspection

self-control, developing, 15–16, 62–63, 78–79, 101, 105, 108, 110, 137–38, 130, 145

self-esteem, *see* inferiority complex

self-improvement, 41n., 63–64, 100, 101, 103, 111, 114, 116, 119, 120, 122, 123, 128, 142, 201–02; by learning from life's experiences, 13, 14; through meditation, 6; using affirmations for, 41

Self-realization, definition of, 6, 206

service to others, 79–80, 80, 84, 129

sex, right attitude toward, 158–59

Shankara, Swami, 18

simple living, 94, 196, 197

sin, right attitude toward, 62–63, 106, 110 ff.

sincerity, soul-quality of, 37–38, 40, 63, 111, 138, 146, 163–64

smile, power of, 13, 37–38, 97, 122–23, 138–39, 184

sorrow, overcoming, 54, 65, 96, 104–05, 105, 114n., 121 ff., 133–34, 172–73, 174–75, 209

soul, man's true Self, 19, 31, 52, 57, 109–110, 112, 113, 114, 122, 140, 154, 178–81, 186–87; immortality of, 167, 168; made in God's image, 4, 5, 152, 181 ff.; nature of, 4, 5, 19, 108, 125, 130, 154, 182, 189 ff.; perceived in meditation, 5; seeing others as, 151; untouched by outer circumstances, 46, 56, 111–12, 170n., 184

spiritual eye, 22, 23, 25, 25n., 29, 188, 190. *See also* Christ center

Sri Yukteswar, Swami, 34, 43, 65, 97, 111, 144, 150, 152, 163, 171, 172, 195, 229, 231, 234

stress, *see* nervousness

success, principles of achieving, 13, 14, 58, 59, 65, 67 ff., 73, 74, 76 ff., 81, 82, 85, 127, 196, 208

suffering, overcoming, 18, 19, 21 ff., 51, 55, 70, 89–90, 92, 103–04, 110–11, 122, 130–31, 144, 169; cause of, 14, 16, 83; purpose of,

14 ff.; right attitude toward, 15–16
superconsciousness, 18–19, 31,
40 ff., 76, 92
sympathy, *see* compassion

temptation, overcoming, 104 ff.
thoughts, fundamental structure of creation, 101–02.
See also mind, attitude,
and positive thinking
truth, nature of, 56, 63,

understanding others, 137, 138.
See also wisdom
unselfishness, 50, 51, 82, 83,
129, 141, 150, 155, 161. *See
also* service to others

visualization, creative use of,
69, 77, 96, 128, 176

war, *see* peace (world)
will power, 39, 67 ff., 76, 77,
106, 107, 126–27, 128;
in overcoming habits,
104–05; key to success, 67
wisdom, cultivating and expressing, 6, 13, 14, 15, 20,
50, 51, 57, 59, 93, 104, 105,
106, 119, 124, 143, 153,
193, 205
work, right attitude toward, 39,
54, 78 ff., 89, 200, 201
worry, overcoming, 32, 35, 54,
55, 58, 70, 87, 89, 91 ff.,

yoga, science of divine communion, 5, 19–20, 26, 53,
54, 64, 98n., 101, 200, 206,
207–08. *See also* meditation *and Kriya Yoga*